Sunshine on Leith

SUNSHINE ON LEITH
HIBERNIAN'S FINEST SONS

Simon Pia

MAINSTREAM
PUBLISHING
EDINBURGH AND LONDON

First published in Great Britain in 1995 by
MAINSTREAM PUBLISHING COMPANY (EDINBURGH) LTD
7 Albany Street
Edinburgh EH1 3UG

ISBN 1 85158 797 7

A catalogue record for this book is available from the British Library

Typeset in Palatino
Printed and bound in Great Britain by Butler & Tanner Ltd, Frome

Dedicated to the memory of Kenny McLean.

CONTENTS

FOREWORD

CHARLIE REID of
THE PROCLAIMERS

Well, how did you feel? I know how I felt when Keith Wright beat Andy Rhodes to score on that glorious afternoon when I finally saw Hibs lift a major trophy. More importantly, how did Keith feel? This book supplies the answers about the good, the bad and the ugly memories of some of our greatest players.

Looking through the names mentioned here I am inspired by just how good the best Hibs players have been. From the Famous Five through Baker, Stanton, Cormack and Cropley down to the current team our players have been among the finest of their generation.

I suppose it was inevitable that I would become a Hibs fan. It was the early '70s and Hibernian were playing the most stylish, attacking football in Scotland. Mind you, getting to the games was going to be a problem – we were living in England. Anyway, while back in Scotland on holiday I saw Hibs beat St Johnstone 7–1 and that was it. Those 90 minutes, the goals, that old terracing that rose up to the clouds. The whole afternoon left such an impression on me that nothing – relegation, not sad Cup exits or even Wallace Mercer could destroy the memory of what I had seen. So, when the going got tough I kept going, and always at the back of my mind there's been the feeling that Hibs' potential is bigger than any of us realise. When the football has been of a high standard Hibs have attracted huge crowds.

In the last few years I have had some justification for my eternal optimism. There is a feeling of quality and stability around the club again. We don't seem to carry passengers any more and while money is as tight as ever some of the youngsters coming through, such as Tweed, Harper and Gardiner, make me believe Hibs can still produce potential internationalists.

I wonder if the guys featured in this book realise how much

their efforts have meant to us all? They have been our personal representatives on the sporting field – our champions. I know I could never feel the same way about Edinburgh if the Hibs weren't there. Love is what it comes down to really.

As you raise your eyes to the new stands, think about the real architects of our new stadium – you and me and guys like these who went the extra mile for us year after year. Gentlemen, thank you.

McEwan Decor

Willie McEwan, managing director, is a well-kent face at Easter
Road and is responsible for grooming the support of the future
as the man behind the highly successful Hibs Kids Club.

Willie's greatest memory is the League Cup triumph in 1972
when Hibs beat Celtic 2–1. His all-time favourite, Pat Stanton,
scored one of the goals in the famous 2–1 victory. Willie never
misses a game and indeed postponed his honeymoon to Paris in
1995 as it clashed with the Scottish Cup semi-final replay with
Celtic.

XILE Clothing

Pat O'Flaherty, the proprietor, was born and bred in Leith. He
recalls being taken as a boy to Easter Road with his father and
passed over heads to his favourite spot down at the front of the
terracing. Pat has great memories of glorious European nights
and his all-time hero Joe Baker, but like Willie, his most
memorable game is the 1972 League Cup final. Pat has recently
introduced his five-year-old son Joe to the delights of watching
Hibs. XILE sponsors Darren Jackson and is frequented by many
of the current team.

Carricknowe Building Services Ltd

Kenny McLean, the managing director, is well known for his
allegiance to the club. He has followed Hibs all over Europe
and, along with his late father Kenny snr, was a leading light in
the 'Hands off Hibs' campaign in 1990. Pat Stanton is his all-
time favourite and the 7–0 demolition of Hearts on New Year's
Day 1973 is his most memorable game. Soon after that game
Kenny bought himself a solid gold '7–0' ring which he still
proudly wears.

Hibernian Supporters Association

The Supporters Association clubroom has been situated at Sunnyside off Easter Road for the last 25 years. Membership is made up of over 2000 supporters from all over the world including branches in Australia, Canada and South Africa. There have been many memorable nights in the clubroom over the years such as victorious parties after the League Cup triumphs in 1972 and 1991 and the night Hibs were saved from an attempted takeover bid by Hearts.

Calor Gas

Calor Gas have been Hibs' shirt sponsors since 1994. Gavin Tomlinson, their regional sales manager, is a fanatical Hibs supporter. He vaguely recalls his first match against Raith Rovers in the early '60s when he arrived five minutes late and left five minutes early, missing both goals in the 1–1 draw

Apart from the League Cup triumphs, Gavin's favourite game was the 0–0 draw with Leeds at Elland Road in a UEFA Cup tie in 1973 when Tony Higgins was the man of the match. Peter Cormack and Des Bremner were other favourites, but top man of them all for Gavin was Jimmy O'Rourke.

ACKNOWLEDGEMENTS

Simon Pia is especially grateful to Graeme Cadger for all his help and assistance.

He also thanks Scotsman Publications Ltd (*Evening News* and *Scotland on Sunday* sports desks) and the Hibs Matchday Programme for permission to reproduce their photographs in the book and on the cover.

HIBERNIAN F.C. SUPPORTERS' ASSOCIATION

11 Sunnyside
Edinburgh EH7 5RA
Tel: 0131 661 3157

INTRODUCTION

This book was the idea of Graeme Cadger who is even more Hibs daft than I am. He thought it would be good to get favourite players from the past and present and hear what they have to say about playing for Hibs and all that entails.

We sat down together and drew up a purely personal list from each era since the '50s that struck a special chord with the fans – well, Graeme and me anyway. They are not necessarily the 18 best players, although some of them undoubtedly are, but the very mention of their names and you think green and white.

We have let the players speak for themselves and give a general impression of life in a Hibs strip. From it you can see this famous old club of ours will always be a special part of their lives. Football may be a profession and there is no reason why it should be more than a job for anyone, but for these men in this book it was. Some of them were born to be Hibs supporters while others have had it thrust upon them as honorary Hibbies for life once they pulled that jersey over their head for the first time.

Not long ago at Joe Baker's testimonial dinner in Edinburgh, Craigie Veitch, the doyen of after-dinner speakers said: 'One thing about you Hibbies is you always look after your heroes.'

Coming from a Jambo that was a big compliment. We believe Hibs fans do care. However, too often in football players are cast aside and forgotten by clubs once the whistle has blown for the last time. It would be nice to think that with the redevelopment of Easter Road and the new club museum, permanent records could be kept by Hibs to honour players who have won the hearts of Hibbies everywhere.

While no man is bigger than the club, no club is bigger than the men who play for it. So this in our own small way is some sort of recognition to players who have made all our trips to

Easter Road over the years that bit special. They did it their way, now they have their say.

CHAPTER ONE

THE PRINCE OF WINGERS

Johnstone was braw, Reilly an' 'aw, but the cocky wee Gordon
was the pride of them 'aw.

Gordon Smith that is, the prince of wingers, and undoubtedly
the most gifted of the Famous Five, the best British forward line
since the war. The prince was in fact neither cocky nor wee, but
was tall, dark and handsome with more than his fair share of self-
effacing modesty. But even in those more reserved times Gordon
was adored by the fans in the '40s and '50s.

As his teammate and long-time friend Lawrie Reilly explains:
'Gordon was a thoroughbred. Even when we knew he wasn't
having a good game he looked wonderful, like an artist, and the
fans loved him no matter what he did. But the rest of us could
never get away with it.'

But it is amazing to think that the prince who turned Easter
Road into a field of dreams for those lucky enough to have seen
him play could well have ended up at Tynecastle instead.

Just like Lawrie a few years later Hearts showed an interest in
me first. I played for a juniors select against a Hibs/Hearts select
in the opening of Lochee Harps ground back in 1941 when I was
16. I scored three and the next day in the *Daily Express* there was
a piece saying that I had signed for Hearts. I could not understand it as I had actually signed nothing, but if it was in the
papers I thought it must be true. My club Dundee North End
explained that Hearts were interested in having me down for a
trial. Then on the Sunday the man from the lemonade factory
next door in Montrose said there was a Mr McCartney on the
phone. I didn't know any Mr McCartney but he asked to meet
me at the Seaforth Hotel in Arbroath. Later I thought the so-and-
so could have come all the way to Montrose if he really wanted
to see me. But anyway I was immediately impressed by the
charisma of the Hibs manager and took an instant liking to him.

He told me Hibs didn't need to give me a trial. He could see with his own eyes that it was not necessary. It was this that had clinched it for me. I never did like trials and even in later years felt I was on trial with Scotland. Mr McCartney also assured me Hibs would look after me and the next day I would be playing for Hibs against Hearts of all people. How could I refuse such an offer?

It was the Edinburgh holiday the next day and I made my debut along with Bobby Combe who I had played with as a schoolboy internationalist. Bobby and I were to become great friends and he was a vital part of Hibs' success over the years and moved up from half back to slot in for one of the Famous Five whenever anyone was injured. I scored a hat trick playing as a centre forward and Bobby got one in a 5–3 victory.

But one of the biggest disappointments of my football career followed shortly after when I got dropped for the final of the Summer Cup against Rangers. Hibs won 3–2 and Jimmy Caskie, just signed from Everton, was picked ahead of me. I had after all only been at Hibs for six weeks while Caskie was a well-known player. But I was in the team that beat Rangers 8–1 in the league the following September. It was a wonderful result especially as Rangers were desperate to get revenge for losing the Summer Cup. From then on over the years we had the edge on Rangers. We had a superiority complex towards them. Most teams dreaded going to Ibrox but we looked forward to it. Somebody pointed out to me that in the 14 league games from the end of the war until we won the league in 1951, we lost only two matches out of 14 against them. They were great contests that gripped the imagination of the whole of Scotland as they were a contrast in styles. Rangers had their 'Iron Curtain' defence whereas Hibs were always all about attack. I suppose that was the real big match during my career.

I actually started at centre forward for Hibs but they thought I would get more protrection on the wing and more space. That was fine by me and over the years I was to play for Scotland in every position in the forward line except for the number 10 spot. Part of the reason I could play either left or right was that as a boy in Montrose an older fellow had told me to just wear a boot on the left foot and a sand shoe on the right. The ball was like a brick in those days and could be blooming sore. So I went from strength to strength with my left over a two to three month period and I remember scoring my first goal with my left foot and feeling it was a great achievement.

I was well looked after in those early days at Hibs especially by Sir Matt Busby and Willie Finnegan. Sir Matt was a phenomenal player and a unique person. He only won two caps but deserved many more. Everyone knew him as one of the lads but he was respected in a special way. Once, coming back from a game things were getting noisy at the back of the bus with a lot of bad language. Sir Matt got up, went down to the back and told the boys to cut it out. And they did immediately. Not many people could get away with doing that with a group of footballers. Years later when it came to my testimonial there was only one choice for me. It had to be Matt and Manchester United. Hibs wanted it to be Arsenal but I held firm for Matt. It was a great occasion as both clubs had just won their respective championships. The amazing thing was that although the score was 7–3 for us it could have gone either way. We played all the top English clubs over the years and nearly always got the better of them.

Just before the end of the war in 1944 I won my first cap against England at Wembley when I was 19, but we lost 6–2. Over the years the papers used to play up rivalry between Willie Waddell and myself for a Scotland place. I never felt I should be preferred to Willie and had watched him win his first cap a couple of years before in a 5–4 win against England at Hampden. But I don't think the Rangers fans liked it very much and I used to get a fair amount of abuse from them whenever I went to Ibrox. I remember one occasion when I was annoyed by Bob Kingsley in the *Sunday Mail*. He was Rangers daft and criicised me for making a gesture at the Ibrox support. I took him to task for it because all I had done was raise my fingers to my lips to tell them to shoosh as I went to take a corner. They were a real rough crowd and were hurling abuse at me. Years later the *Evening Times* ran a piece about Willie Waddell and me and pointed out I had won more caps, 18 compared to his 17. I got on the phone to Willie to joke about it as we were goods friends. We had a rare laugh but you should have heard his language as he swore like a trooper.

In the years after the war we got better as a team and it was only a matter of time before we won our first League championship in 1948. But one thing we could never do over the years was win the cup. It definitely became psychological. Year after year we came so close but it just seemed impossible and we were beaten by all sorts of teams. We lost the first post-war final after beating Rangers and Motherwell. Cubby (Johnny Cuthbertson) scored in the first minute of the final against Aberdeen but we failed to hold on. The next season we got our revenge and I remember it well. I was captain and we lost Willie Ormond with a broken leg and Jimmy Kerr with a fractured hand in the first half. Down to nine men I felt it was time to do something and ran from my half right through the middle to put us 2–1 up. At half time we decided to bring Jimmy back on although he could only use one hand. We knew we had better keep the play well away from him which we did. We won 4–2 but finally lost in the semi-finals. Jimmy never quite recovered from the injury which was a shame because he was invincible that season.

That season I scored five goals in a league game against Third Lanark with Alex Linwood getting the other three as we won 8–0. It's a record I believe I share with Joe Baker who also scored a record nine in the cup against Peebles Rovers in the Cup. But to be truthful I don't think I played particularly well that day. I have played far better and never scored. A point I like to make is that most goals are actually made by somebody and credit is not given enough to the creator, just the scorer. The next time we won the league in 1950/51 we had another epic with Aberdeen in the League Cup. We lost 4–1 at Pittodrie and I had injured my hamstring. Coming back on the train I said I wanted to play in the second leg. My relationship with Hibs was such that they would let me decide. They had faith in me and I spoke to Sir John Bruce (the Hibs director who was a surgeon at the Western General) about it. He thought it was impossible but told me to try and gently run it off. It was very painful but gradually over the next few days I could move a bit but not quickly. Sir John Bruce was astonished I could run at all. But it was agreed I would play as it would give us a psychological edge. I went into the dressing-room 15 minutes before kick-off and began to strip. The boys thought I was joking. It had all been a big secret between Hugh Shaw and myself. We heard a huge roar from the crowd when it was announced over the tannoy I would be playing.

Aberdeen's captain and left back was Davie Shaw who had been at Hibs for years and when I went up to shake his hand I gave him a triumphant look. That was him beat. I am not trying to be boastful but there and then we had won the game. We went on to lead 4–0 and, as the gloamin came down, Yorston grabbed one back for Aberdeen. So it was through to Ibrox where we drew 1–1, but the next day we won 5–1 in the second play-off, this time at Hampden. It was in the game at Ibrox I had my worst ever miss. The ball came over from the left and I side-footed it onto the crossbar. It was 1–1 at the time and I'll never forget it. After that I learned never to criticise. Anyone can miss. Unfortunately we again lost in the final that year, this time to Motherwell.

Although Sir John Bruce was amazed at my recovery for the Aberdeen game, he used to ridicule me about my own treatment. I used to go down to the beach at Portobello and paddle in the salt water. Jimmy McColl, our trainer, was keen on horses and told me about racehorses getting this treatment. I thought it worked a treat. It was just like an aerotone with the ice cold, the salt and the ripple. But Sir John Bruce always claimed it was psychological. I did get a fair amount of clattering over my career and we did get less protection than players do today. I fractured my tibia against Raith in 1953 and my spell at Hibs ended when Shanks of Airdrie did in the ligaments on my ankle. That was an accident, but I remember once some boys warned me that a fellow called McLaren who played for Raith was going about saying he would break my leg. He did try his best but never succeeded.

Not long after the five against Third Lanark I had another couple of games that stand out. We went to Ibrox and they were having a right go at me as usual, so I thought I would make them wheesh. I scored two, shooting one in from the byline which caught Bobby Brown by surprise as it was almost an impossible angle. I then caught him out again from 40 yards. But the goal I liked best in that game was one Cubby scored. I beat Tiger Shaw and the rest of the Rangers defence playing keepie-uppie and then lobbed the ball over for Cubby to shoot in. We won 4–2 that day, but the keepie-uppie was something I tried a lot and I was not meaning to be immodest. Most players can do it practising on their own so why not have a go in a game, I say. However today your manager would probably give you a hard time and substitute you. You've got to pass all the time but is that what people really want to see all the time? Even then Hughie Shaw would give me a hard time of it. Jimmy McColl would give me the ball at training and I would lap the park keeping it up and Hugh would shout at me to ask why I was wasting my time as I could do it already. I tried to make him understand that continual practice perfected your skill. Training in those days did not concentrate on the ball enough. I particularly hated the medicine ball and could not see what it had to do with football. One day I broke my finger with it. It's still knackered to this day. I wrapped it up with a big bandage and made sure Hugh Shaw noticed it at one of our team talks. When he found out how it happended he never went on at me about it again.

An old fellow was reminding me recently of how I played keepie-uppie regularly even when I played for Scotland. I don't think some of the selectors approved. Anyway he reminded me of the time at Easter Road I ran the ball up my shin just inside our half in a match against Rangers. I then flicked it up with my knee on to my head and set off down the slope, keeping it up with my head. The blasted thing was that when I got into their goalmouth I headed just past. I did it again shortly after that game against poor old Third Lanark. I juggled it with my head but when it got to the final header it went too close to the goal-keeper. I had scored like this as a schoolboy and it was a big regret I never got one like that as a professional.

It was around this time that the Famous Five came together, but to be honest we never really noticed it at the time. There were many other fine players such as Alec Linwood, Johnny Cuthbertson, Willie Finnegan and Bobby Combe. Already Eddie Turnbull and Willie Ormond had been in the team for a few years and Lawrie was starting to make his mark – mind you as a left winger originally – and Bobby Johnstone had joined the club.

I was the old stager of the Five as I had been at Hibs eight years. Maybe I was first to catch on that we were something special. Sometimes I had played at centre forward but I didn't play like other number 9s. I would come back to pick the ball up and played deep, facing my own goal a lot of the time. All the time I believed in moving about the field which the others did as well. As a winger I would drop way back to pick the ball up on our 18 yard line. I had Tommy Younger well trained to give it to me. At that time most number 7s waited to get service from the right half. But what this forward line had was a mixture of styles.

Bobby Johnstone was what I would call a pure footballer. He himself didn't know what he was going to do next so the opposition had no chance. He was a grand player. I had a partnership with him and he was adept at moving the ball from foot to foot. Inside Bobby was Lawrie. What can you say? He was the master goal scorer. He was more than that as well but if you wanted goals galore Lawrie was your man.

Eddie was the powerhouse, a strong player with an incredible shot. He'd run back after one of his thunderbolts and I'd say 'Good effort Eddie' and he'd reply: 'Must have a pop.'

Then there was Willie, a straightforward winger who was very fast. He had only one foot but it did him no harm – just like Puskas. You can get away with being one-footed if you can play like Willie.

But the main thing about our understanding was running into position. A lot more teams do it today but then nobody did it. But we did it all the time. It can be devastating and if you're getting to the ball first all the time and in space the confidence of the opposition begins to go.

The big regret I have about that team was that the European Cup didn't start until the mid-'50s. If it had been in the early '50s I am convinced Hibs would have won it. The two years we won the league we were an outstanding team who could have beaten anyone. By the time we played in the first European Cup we were a bit past it and Bobby Johnstone had been transferred to Manchester City.

Hibs had been pioneers going out into Europe. The wee chairman, Harry Swan, had great vision in that respect. He'd got McCartney from Hearts and each year after the war we would go on tours to Sweden, Denmark, Austria, Germany, France and even Brazil. The first day we went down on to the Copacabana, in 1952, I thought they were playing netball. As I got nearer I saw they were keeping the ball up with their bare feet. I was just a novice compared to what I saw these kids doing. I think we were the first team from Britain to realise just how great Brazil were going to be. We played three games, drawing two and losing one. I heard later that Vasco da Gama, the Brazilian champions, were interested in buying me and Bobby Johnstone. I was very flattered to think that they would want me. The French club Cannes also made enquiries after we had played them and looking back it might have been a worthwhile experience playing abroad but to be honest I was more than happy at Easter Road. And I did not think there were better teams than Hibs around at that time.

Going abroad you learned a lot of things especially how old

fashioned our football could be. Our press would blame the ball or the state of the pitch abroad for British teams losing, but the balls we played with were too hard. You couldn't squeeze your thumbs into them. The balls they used abroad were undoubtedly superior as was the footwear.

On one tour Adidas supplied us with boots with moulded soles, not the usual studs. A German team had been good enough to tell us we had been wearing the wrong boots against them. They were a real godsend. The difference was like night and day. How could you dribble on frosty grounds in Scotland with studs? That was why I used to wear basketball shoes.

My international career spanned over 13 years with Scotland, but I always felt that the selectors' hearts weren't in it as far as I was concerned. My happiest period playing for Scotland was when we went on a tour of Austria, Hungary and Yugoslavia in 1955. It was due to a wee fluke that I became captain when George Young pulled out with an injury. It was a great honour and I felt it was a vote of confidence in me. As I have said, too often I felt I was on trial, but I really enjoyed that tour. The old guard in the Scotland team had been broken up after a disastrous performance at Wembley and they had got rid of the cliques. I had been recalled for a 3–0 win over Portugal at Hampden before we set off. We drew with Yugoslavia 2–2, beat Austria 4–1 and lost to Hungary 3–1. The game in Austria is memorable for a near riot I almost caused. Their full back fouled me and usually I jumped up immediately so that they did not think they had got the better of me. This time I was slower than usual and as he went to give me a hand I shouted at him to leave me alone and waved my fist at him. That got the crowd going and some tried to invade the pitch but luckily the police stopped them. I got my first international goal against Yugoslavia and scored another in Austria. However, the Hungarians were too good for us and they had a marvellous side with Puskas, Hidgekuti and co. This was the team that had been to the World Cup final and had annihilated England at Wembley two years before. After such a good tour I was delighted to see Hibs take part in the first European Cup. But as I have said it came four years too late. Kopa was brilliant for Reims and if they hadn't had him we would have won without a doubt and gone on to meet Real Madrid. Now that would have been some game. I played in Scotland's World Cup qualifying games for 1958, but injury ruled out any chance I would have of playing in the finals.

Looking back now I don't blame Hibs for letting me go the following season. They obviously thought I was too old and would not be the same after such an injury and operation. I went to Sir John Bruce who was a rabid Hibs fan. I took it for granted Hibs would accept his verdict that I would be okay to play on. But the wee chairman said that the operation would do me more harm than good, prolonging my career. Whether he really believed it is another matter. Deep down I was very hurt when Hibs finally announced I could go. The next morning, a Sunday at 8 a.m., I got a call from who else but my old sparring partner for the Scotland jersey Willie Waddell. He wanted me to come to Kilmarnock. I've always appreciated that call, but it was too far for me to travel on a daily basis, but I got quite a shock who came in for me next. It was unthinkable to me that I would ever play for Hearts. No one in Scotland disliked Hearts more than me. What else would you expect from someone under the influence of Messrs McCartney, McColl and Shaw for 18 years?

I was a professional and had to earn a living. It was not the best kept secret that I couldn't be too bothered to begin with and dreaded in a way the reception I would get but I have to say the club and Hearts supporters were marvellous to me. More than that I took great comfort from the Hibs fans' response. They were on my side. They wrote to the papers and sent me letters personally. Not one Hibs fan criticised me. I did feel the club should have waited till after the operation and given me one last chance to see if it had succeeded. But that was it and I must admit it was strange going back to play against the green and white. I did win two more league medals with Hearts and Dundee and got to the semi-finals of the European Cup again with Dundee. Not many people are aware that I also had a short spell with Morton as well and Irish club Drumcondra before I called it a day just a month before my fortieth birthday. I had played another five years and always felt I could have given these to Hibs.

CHAPTER TWO

GIE THE BA' TAE REILLY

Speak to Lawrie Reilly for a few minutes and you soon get an idea why Gordon Smith called him the master goal scorer. He's direct, to the point and there's no messing about. The ideal temperament for a striker. No room for doubts and not a moment's hesitation, just go for it. Lawrie's style comes across in his attitude to his nickname 'Last Minute Reilly'.

'Ach, it was a load of nonsense. Just newspaper talk. The *Sunday Express* once worked out I had scored 19 last-minute goals. But what about all the goals I got, say in the 44th or 46th minute. It was just because I scored on the whistle that people noticed and it happened on such a famous occasion at Wembley in 1953. But I always played to the whistle, like any pro should, so there was nothing special about it. Maybe the only difference between me and some others was that if there was five minutes to go I never let my head go down. I thought I was just as likely to score then as any time. Too few people forget it only takes a second to stick one in.'

And stick them in he did. Such was Lawrie's lethal reputation that the legendary cry from the Easter Road terraces 'Gie the ba' tae Reilly' struck fear into defenders.

Lawrie's goalscoring feats made him Hibs' top League goal scorer of all time with 187 and his total of 234 in league and cup competitions makes him the leading post-war goalscorer. Lawrie is also the most capped Hibs player of all time with a total of 38 matches and 22 goals. Only SFA ineptitude in 1950 and illness in 1954 denied him the chance to play for Scotland in the World Cup.

Who's to say Reilly would not have notched up some record in that competition? But when it comes to his career, one of the main things Lawrie is only too keen to point out is he was the only one of the Famous Five who was born and bred a Hibs supporter.

My family were all daft about Hibs and my father, Jimmy, who worked on the railways took me with my mother all over Scotland to see Hibs. The fact that I grew up in Bryson Road near Tynecastle only made me even more of a Hibs supporter. As a young lad one of my heroes was none other than Gordon Smith. Gordon is four years five months older than me which is a big gap in your teens. So when he joined Hibs I was 13. I even remember going up to Gordon and inviting him to my house for a cup of tea as he walked along Ardmillan after his debut when Hibs beat Hearts 5–3. Gordon must have thought I was just a daft young laddie and he was probably right, but needless to say in years to come he was to take up the offer. Little did I know then that four years later I would be playing alongside him at Easter Road. I'll always be grateful to Harry Reading for tipping off Hibs manager Willie McCartney about me. Playing for North Merchiston and Edinburgh Thistle, clubs began to show an interest and when Dave McLean the Hearts manager came into the picture Harry got on to Easter Road immediately. Willie McCartney did not hang around and invited me and my dad down. He could have offered me anything and we would have accepted.

It's funny but I joined Hibs as a right winger while Gordon was at centre forward. A switch in roles would be one of the essential pieces in the jigsaw that made up the Famous Five.

I made my debut a week before I was 17 against Kilmarnock and was a fringe player when Hibs won the league in 1947/48 season. But at the start of the next season I got seven games on the left wing after Willie Ormond broke his leg. My form was such that I won my first call-up for Scotland. When Willie returned I moved inside to centre forward and the spot remained my own for the next decade.

When the Famous Five came together at the start of season 1948/49 it was something that just happened. Willie McCartney has to take credit for signing all of us, but there were a lot of good players around Easter Road in that era. However, this one proved to be the perfect formula. I was the odd man out so to speak while the wingers and inside forwards complemented each other perfectly.

Willie and Gordon were a total contrast. Willie was fast and direct and liked the ball pushed in front of him as he raced up the wing to whip in his crosses. Gordon, though, liked the ball at his feet and then you'd marvel at the things he could do with it. He was the closest thing to Stanley Matthews I've ever seen. Gordon was captain at the time and led by example. There was no need for any bawling. Eddie Turnbull was a powerful grafter of an inside left with a thunderbolt of a shot. Inside on my right Bobby Johnstone was a classic Scottish inside forward with bags of skill. 'Nicker' got his name from Black Bob in the *Sunday Post* who had a Selkirk collie of that name.

Playing with such players was a pleasure and I refer to them as the Famous Four. I was there in the middle to take advantage of all their work. I never considered myself that good in the air so both Willie and Gordon would fire over balls about five feet in the air or under. Gordon would chip it in time and again to the near post as he knew that's where I wanted it. There were never any of these high floating balls you see so often these days, a sign a forward line don't know what they are doing.

The only shouting we ever did between ourselves was for the ball. The service these players gave meant you could not fail to score. Gordon, especially, knew exactly when to give it to you. There is nothing worse in football than going into space and not getting the right pass. When you got in the right position with the Famous Four you knew damn well you would get it.

I have heard Denis Law and Bobby Charlton moan about George Best and not getting the ball from him at the right time. The same was said about Jinky Johnstone, but you could never say that about Gordon. To me that is the true sign of a great player. You see the man in position and you make sure he gets it and 99 times out of 100 that happened with us.

There was harmony off the pitch and everyone had their own space. Gordon was always very much a loner or palled around with Bobby Combe and we respected that. But on away trips Willie, Eddie, Nicker and myself would play cards while Gordon sat and read. Socially Willie, Eddie and Nicker palled around together and were partial to a wee refreshment. They were also the three comedians in the team. I remember one game at New Year we turned up to take the train to Falkirk. The carriage smelled like a brewery and these three looked really rough but we still went out and won 5–1. My particular mates were other teetotallers like John Paterson and Archie Buchanan.

While it was Willie McCartney who brought the Famous Five together, Hugh Shaw was in charge after McCartney died. There were some tactics but not a lot. We just knew how each other played. We moved into space for each other and passed at the right time. While I have referred to the Famous Four I probably would just as well be calling it the Famous Six as Bobby Combe was an important part of it all. He had moved to half-back to accommodate Bobby Johnstone, but could move into any position in the forward line if someone was injured. Bobby Combe was in the Eddie Turnbull mould and to be fair his presence never really weakened the team.

After games we would sit in the boardroom and discuss our mistakes. There was a tremendous atmosphere at Easter Road and I loved it so much I would go in early for training. We would set up a net in the dressing-room and play badminton or juggle the ball around. We would lark around as well and if someone had made a mistake on Saturday and given away a goal we would buy a leek and stick it in their coat pocket.

Looking back on that period when we won three league championships in 1947/48, 1950/51 and 1951/52 my only regret is that Hibs never won the Cup. God just didn't want it. It was such a big thing to win the Cup then. The league was not as important as it is today what with the European Cup. But with the Cup you could come back and parade through the streets of Edinburgh. We got close on many occasions but kept failing in the semi-finals. There was the classic game against Motherwell when we lost John Ogilvie early on then Willie Ormond went off with a broken leg and we finally lost 3–2.

But Rangers were our main rivals at that time. It was a case of the Iron Curtain versus the Famous Five. It was often suggested it would make an ideal Scotland team, but it never happened although I think it would have been a good idea. It was also a shame that the Famous Five never lined up together for Scotland. We were all capped but the closest we came was when Smith, Johnstone, Reilly and Ormond lined up to face the League of Ireland in 1952, but Billy Steele of Motherwell kept out Eddie. It would have been nice to have had Eddie in the team and you can be sure Turnbull would not have let Scotland down.

Lawrie's international career compares favourably with two other all time greats – Denis Law and Kenny Dalglish. Both scored 30 goals for Scotland, but Lawrie's tally of 22 works out at .57 goals per game – a better average than Denis Law's average of .54. As for Kenny Dalglish his average was less than one in three games.

As well as there being far fewer internationals in those days Lawrie also had the bad luck to miss out on the World Cup in 1954 due to pleurisy.

I well remember how and where I heard about my first international honour. It also gives a fair idea of how a footballer's life style has changed since then. I was waiting at the bus stop in Dundee Street – no sponsored cars in those days – on my way to play Manchester United in a testimonial for Willie McCartney's widow at Easter Road. A neighbour stopped and congratulated me on being capped. I didn't know what he was talking about but he said it was in the stop press section of the papers. I was tempted to dash back to the house but headed on down to Easter Road. I got off at Boswell Street and there were the queues stretching back onto Easter Road. People were patting me on the back congratulating me so I knew it must be true.

I scored twice in a 5–1 win over the League of Ireland and less than a month later I made my full international debut against Wales. In my first 12 internationals Scotland won every game and Wembley proved a happy hunting ground for me. I scored five times in five appearances there. Any player who cannot be inspired by Wembley should not be playing the game, especially a Scotsman. To walk out of the tunnel with the huge Scotland support was something special.

My international career made me a favourite with fans all over Scotland due to my feats against the Auld Enemy such as the double in 1953 at Wembley when Scotland were down to ten men.

Other teams' supporters were great to me and a lot of it had to do with the fact that everybody liked Hibs so much because we were such an entertaining team. I even got a good reception at Ibrox although I can't say the same for Gordon. They saw him as a rival to Willie Waddell in the right wing spot. But despite Rangers' influence Gordon won one more cap than Willie. I must say there's no city like Glasgow for football and even when I had finished playing people would stop me in the street.

Fans in those days reacted differently to another team scoring. They'd applaud a really good goal, something I'll do to this day bar for a Hearts one. Some people think my best goal was one against Falkirk, but that would be because it was at Easter Road so more Hibs supporters saw it. But I'd go for one against Motherwell. Saying that, the Falkirk one was not bad. Eddie

Turnbull thundered over a shot from the right and I instinctively stuck out my head and the ball flew into the net. Bobby Brown in Falkirk's goal never smelled it. He just stood there and clapped. It was a bit of a fluke, but I did catch it perfectly and it just about took the net away. It was like returning a 120 mph service at tennis.

But with the Motherwell goal I did everything right. We had been leading 4–1, but they pulled back to 4–3. Motherwell were getting on top and as I moved back to the halfway line I picked up our keeper's clearance. I nodded it over their centre-half, beat their half-back and set off down the park. I must have gone round five players and then I walked it round their keeper and tapped it in. Even the home fans applauded it and whenever I went back to Fir Park their fans always gave me a great ovation. Not long ago some older Motherwell fans reminded me of it and described it as being like that famous Jimmy Greaves goal, but they said it was even better. I don't know, but to be truthful Motherwell made it easier for me that day as they all dived in to the tackle. There's nothing a forward likes more, believe me. If they had tried to jockey me it might have been a bit different.

However, I really appreciated the way the Motherwell fans reacted and I feel fans should always applaud a great goal when they see one. However, as I've said, there are exceptions, such as any Hearts goal. I could never applaud one of them.

A special match that stands out for me was the 3–2 cup victory over Rangers in 1952. It was the quarter final at Ibrox and there was a huge crowd. Bobby Johnstone got the winner. After that we thought the Cup was ours, but once again it was not to be.

Another game I remember which was nowhere near as glamorous was a match at Brockville. We were 3–0 down and I was glaring down the pitch at the defence every time Falkirk scored. I could see Jock Govan thinking 'There's that wee bastard, Reilly giving us that look. I'd like to see him do any better.' But we pulled back to 3–3 and then Tommy Younger gave away a penalty, but somehow we got back and won 5–4. I never scored in that game but it's one I'll never forget.

But there are no doubts about my hat-trick of top three games. One I watched as a young Hibs supporter, one I played in and the other is a more recent game. The first was the 8–1 league victory over Rangers in 1941. Hibs had beaten Rangers a few months before in the Summer Cup, then came the league meeting in September. Gordon and Bobby Combe had only made their debuts at the end of the previous season and Gordon had missed out on the Summer Cup final. But both were in for the league game and Bobby scored four while Gordon and Arthur Milne got two apiece. It was wonderful to watch.

The best game I ever played in was Gordon's testimonial game against Manchester United in September 1952. Hibs were champions of Scotland and they were English champions. Both sides were also renowned for their attacking football.

We were all delighted to see Sir Matt Busby back at Easter Road. Eddie put us ahead then they went 2–1 ahead before Eddie got a penalty. However, United went in 3–2 up at half time. The second half was even better. United missed a penalty, had a goal disallowed and then I had a goal chalked off. Willie Ormond got the equaliser and then Eddie got another penalty. Then Gordon got on the scoresheet, I nabbed a header and Eddie finished off the scoring. Although it finished 7–3 the score could have been anything. That was the sort of football fans wanted to see. Over that era there was a strong connection between Hibs and Manchester United. I had been a laddie when Matt was at Hibs but there was something special about him in those days. He was a thorough gentleman and was like a father figure. A big man in every way. Hibs also had a good relationship with Spurs as well and I well remember a few tussles with Alf Ramsey, but I always got the better of him.

Hibs were way ahead of everyone in those days and were the first team to go on tours after the war in Germany, Austria, France, Belgium and Holland, but one of the most memorable was the Brazilian trip in 1953. We flew out on the day the Queen was crowned and what a horrendous journey it was. We went from Edinburgh to London to Paris then onto Lisbon. From there to Dakar and on to Recife and then Rio. We played the Brazilian champions in the Maracana and the amazing thing is that after a 26-hour journey we somehow managed to get a 2–2 draw against Vasco da Gama and I scored both. It was some experience as there were 30,000 locked out . Although it was their winter it was still hell of a warm. We lost the second and third games, wilting in the heat. The Brazilian style was all possession football and I was bored by half time in the first game I watched and wanted to leave.

It was on account of this foreign travel that we were invited to participate in the inaugural European Cup. Our first game

was against German champions Rot-Weiss Essen and Hugh
Shaw asked Eddie and Bobby Johnstone to lie deep. Now Bobby
couldn't lie deep in two feet of water, but Hugh's idea was to
hold them in Germany. There were a lot of British soldiers there
to cheer us on and after ten to 15 minutes I said to Bobby: 'This
lot aren't that good. I don't know about lying back, let's have a
go.' We won 4–0. They had Helmut Rahn who had scored the
winning goal in the World Cup final against Hungary playing,
but he was not in the same class as Gordon. Djurgaarden were
not much problem in the next round, but Reims were too much
for us. Raymond Kopa was the best player I played against. He
was brilliant and without him we could have beaten Reims and
gone on to meet Real Madrid in the first final.

However, everything was not plain sailing with Hibs and
me. There were problems over a testimonial at the start of
season 1953/54. I wanted it written into my new contract but
Hibs refused. Hugh Shaw did not approve of testimonials and
pointed out Gordon's testimonial had been agreed by Willie
McCartney. So I refused to sign, put in a transfer request and
Hibs let other clubs know they were open to offers. I never
wanted to leave, but thought it was a player's right. Hibs
actually flew me down to see Manchester United and there was
talk that Arsenal and Rangers were interested. I stuck to my
guns and did not play for about four months. I ended up
making more money from newspapers commenting on games
than if I had been playing for Hibs, Sir George Graham of the
SFA intervened and said he would arrange for an international
select to play in a testimonial for me. People said he wanted to
make sure I was available for Scotland so I signed and made my
comeback against Manchester United at Old Trafford in a 2–2
draw. I think I made a point to Hugh Shaw and Harry Swan by
scoring both goals.

I was glad it had all been settled. Hugh Shaw had inherited
a great side at Easter Road from Willie McCartney and the set-
up was second to none. McCartney was a real showman with
his hat, flower in his buttonhole, the wing collar and striped
trousers. He was just like Bertram Mills. He sat in the Stand and
there was none of this patter with telephones as they have
today. He was a strict disciplinarian and told us not to drink but
he had a hard job with some of our players. Wee Harry Swan
was a forward-looking chairman who would have been at home
in the game today, but he knew nothing about football. He

would come down to the dressing-room and give his spiel. As soon as he left McCartney would tell us to forget everything Harry Swan had said and then he told us what he wanted.

But that 1953/54 season only got worse for me when I caught pleurisy playing against Aberdeen in the Cup in February. I was out of the game for months and went on a trip to Denmark to recuperate. I brought back cut-away continental boots with screw in studs which I hoped Hibs would adopt wholescale instead of the tackity boots that were *de rigeur* in Scotland.

I always felt that you shouldn't skimp over such things as a footballer's most vital assets were his feet. It seemed obvious that you should kit them out as well as possible, but I remembered that the previous season I had gone into Thornton's and ordered a pair of Cotton Oxfords for £5. When I took them into Easter Road the trainer Jimmy McColl told me Hugh Shaw wanted to see me. He wanted to know why I had ordered such a pair when I should have got the ones that cost £3.10/-. Believe it or not I was getting a row for it.

I returned from my pleurisy setback in time to play the Mighty Magyars who had just slaughtered England 6–3 at Wembley. A trial match was staged at Brockville. What a night! There were freezing gales full of sleet. It was so cold that at half-time we stripped off our shorts and tops and went in to the showers with our boots on to keep warm. If I could come through that I'd be all right. Puskas, Hidgekuti Bozsik and co won 4–2, but we gave the Hungarians more of a game than England did. A few weeks later England were whipped 7–1 in Budapest. What impressed me in that game was Hidgekuti's deep-lying centre forward role and I thought it would suit me. In my later years with Hibs I got the chance to play that way.

It was a pity my career was cut short at the relatively young age of 29. If I had played on for a few years what a combination we could have had with me in a deep-lying role and Joe Baker running riot.

Sir John Bruce had warned me that I would have a lot of trouble with my knee after he operated on a cyst on my cartilage and to this day my knee is still swollen.

My last game for Hibs was against Rangers in 1958, a week before the Cup final when Hibs lost to Clyde. We beat Rangers as usual and I scored, but I had tonsilitis so I didn't even get to the final. However the best scoring centre forward I have ever seen was waiting to take over. Joe Baker was quite different from me in style but he was so sharp and had a great eye for goal. I don't think I was missed so much because of Joe.

I had to wait a few more years for the most exciting game I've ever seen. It was, believe it or not, on New Year's Day 1973. That 7–0 walloping of Hearts had everything. I loved every minute of it. That was a good Hibs team – the best since my era. They had good defenders. I liked Blackley and Brownlie and the midfield was special with Edwards, Stanton and Cropley. Jimmy O'Rourke and Alan Gordon were ordinary players but they complemented each other so well. Eddie Turnbull got as good a blend as you could which is what it's all about. A team full of Lawrie Reillys and Gordon Smiths would win nothing. Perhaps the problem with that team was that Eddie broke it up too soon, bringing in Joe Harper. He was about three stone overweight when Eddie signed him, but he was wearing a heavy fleece coat. So Eddie was remembering the Joe Harper he knew at Aberdeen and blamed Billy Bingham for pulling a fast one.

Today things are a lot different and I don't think the standard is as good, but for me the top team in Scotland will always be the Hibs.

CHAPTER THREE

THUNDERBALL

In many ways he was the unsung hero of the Famous Five but probably no one has contributed so much to Hibs as Eddie Turnbull. He won three league championship medals over a 12-year playing career and led the club to a League Cup and two Drybrough Cup trophies as manager. His team, 'Turnbull's Tornadoes', has been the best since the Famous Five's. And no doubt they would have won more had they not emerged at the same time as the Lisbon Lions, the most successful club side Scotland has ever had.

At the stage when Eddie took over Hibs, Celtic were topping-up with the likes of Dalglish, McGrain, Hay and Macari. In any other period Turnbull's team would surely have captured a few league titles.

Eddie himself would be the first to admit that he was not the most skilful of the Five, but he had the best football brain. He went on to prove it as a coach and today former players, even those who had their fall-outs with him, will tell you no one knew more about the game than Turnbull. Another little known fact about the man from Carronshore is that he was the first British footballer to score in European competition. This highlight of Eddie's career came in Hibs' 4–0 rout of Rot-Weiss Essen in the inaugural European Cup, but he could so easily have missed out on a football career.

Eddie was demobbed from the Navy in 1946. Portsmouth had shown an interest in him when he played for the Navy in the south of England, but he wanted to get back home. The young Turnbull had stood out at schoolboy level playing alongside George Young and Bobby Brown, but he did not consider a career in football and turned down an offer from Bo'ness United. Eddie recalls:

I was persuaded to lace up for Forth Rangers, a Grangemouth Junior side, as I knew the captain and secretary. In the first game the opponents just happened to be Bo'ness and the score was 2–2. I must have done all right as the local taxi man, Lukie Reid, called at the house later that night. I was in bed but the next morning one of my brothers told me Lukie would be coming round at 5.30 p.m. that evening to take me to Easter Road. To be quite frank, I did not know much about Hibs. Falkirk was the local team and most of us looked towards Glasgow. Tully Craig, a local lad, had played for both of the Old Firm.

Anyway, I went through with my oldest brother to meet Willie McCartney. The manager was some man and as he kept slipping the nips to my brother, he became more and more convinced I should sign for Hibs. So it was sealed there and then and my brother had a good kip on the way home. But I, too, had been won over immediately by McCartney. He was a real entrepreneur and a lovely man. He always wore his homburg hat and a red carnation in his buttonhole. You rarely saw him in the morning as Hughie Shaw and Jimmy McColl took the training, but his presence filled the club. I went full time straightaway and being a country lad stayed in the background at first. I would travel through with Jimmy Cairns and Willie Ormond on the bus. Although Willie lived only five minutes up the road this was the first time we had met.

All the players respected McCartney and there was great harmony at the club, with no cliques. There were a lot of experienced pros such as Willie Finnegan, Sammy Keane, Davie Shaw, Hugh Howie, the master passer Bobby Combe and, of course, Gordon Smith. Gordon wasn't a mixer. He was introverted and did his own thing, but I got on well with him. I enjoyed the camaraderie and the guys liked a half pint and to go to the dancing. I got into the team in my first season after a game against Sparta Prague. My first league game was against Alloa, near by Carronshore, and one of my cousins was right half for them. Not long after I scored my first goal playing at centre forward against Motherwell. John Johnstone, the Motherwell keeper, was a Bo'ness lad I knew and he cleared the ball only as far as Hugh Howie, who nodded it on. I caught it on the volley, a real arsehole winder as we called it in those days, and it ended up in the back of the net. Thus the famous Turnbull thunderbolt made its appearance in Hibs' weaponry.

In my first season we reached the Cup final against Aberdeen. I was so naïve then and just could not believe we could lose. We went ahead through a Johnny Cuthbertson goal after 90 seconds, but we ended up losing 2–1 and Finnegan got his jaw broken. It was the first of many Cup let-downs I had with Hibs. We could do it in the league but when the chips were down in the Cup we often didn't have enough players full of blood and guts. That's what you need in Cup ties and perhaps that was the only weakness in our team and throughout the '50s.

Not long after that we lost in the League Cup final to Motherwell, whereas we had scored 13 goals in our previous two games. But at the start of that season one of Hibs' first games was at Pittodrie. There were 42,000 at the game with the crowd sitting on the track. We took our revenge for the Cup defeat and were on our way to the title.

Willie McCartney had brought all the elements of the Famous Five together but died early in 1948 after a Cup tie versus Albion Rovers. It was a terrible, no-scoring draw in freezing weather on a rutted pitch at Cliftonhill. It all must have been too much for the old boss. And Harry Swan asked if I would go back in the limo with him. We dropped him at his house on Queensferry Road. Later that night, as we came out of the dancing, the news vendors were shouting out 'McCartney's dead'. All the players were devastated. He was such a radiant person. His great gimmick was to come down from the stand for the last fifteen minutes and he would take up the whole tunnel. You certainly started running when you saw him there. He was before his time, using a pool system of players and played all of us in a variety of positions. Perhaps this helped us to interchange so well as the Famous Five.

Gordon Smith was an artist. No other word for it. Every team in Scotland had wingers in those days and he was the best. He had so much skill in both feet and had a great shot. But as well as his dribbling and goal scoring he had real vision in making a pass.

Bobby Johnstone was a silky wee player with tremendous vision, like Gordon. He was so cultured and great at linking the play.

Then there was Lawrie Reilly who was always restless. He never gave defences a minute's peace. You can't teach people what Lawrie Reilly had. His instinct to be in the right place at the right time to knock the ball in was inborn.

Then there was my wee friend Willie Ormond. In those days the *Weekly News* had a football skit, 'Wan Fitted', based on wee

Willie but, by Christ, it was a good one he had. Willie was my room-mate on away trips and Bobby was another pal. If anyone touched Willie or Bobby on the park, I would sort them out. It was something I could not stand. The thing about us was we could all score goals. Everyone would get 20-odd a season. We could all pass it as well. No other team I have seen since then has interchanged the way we did. The five of us would swap in and out of roles, doing each other's when required. No one taught us what we had going between us. But all five of us thought about the game in the same way.

I suppose what people remember about me was that I could clog it. A bit of a thunderbolt they would say. That was due to my upbringing. At the back of our house in Carronshore there was waste ground and a wooden fence which I would rattle the ball against every day. I perfected my timing so I could clock it really well.

The Famous Five's big rivals were Rangers and we really relished playing against them although most teams feared them. But I think Rangers feared us and we quite enjoyed taking the mickey out of them. I suppose the most memorable match for me was when we beat them 3–2 in the Cup quarter-final in 1951 at Ibrox in front of over 100,000. Twice Rangers went ahead, but Gordon got one back and I clocked another. Then we got a free kick 25 yards out with 10 minutes to go. I put the ball down and they all expected me to have a pop, but wee Bobby had gone into the wall between Willie Woodburn and George Young. I clipped the ball nice and firmly to Bobby who flicked it up with his left and then hit a right-footed overhead kick. It was an incredible goal.

One of the things I appreciated most about Hibs was their vision in going on close-season trips to Europe. Chairman Harry Swan and McCartney were forward looking and every year we were away playing in Germany, France, Switzerland, Austria and, of course, there was the trip to Brazil in 1953. We learned an awful lot and we had good laughs along the way. The night before we were due to play Cologne we had a few jars and were getting into a wee bit of dancing in the hotel. There were one or two Cologne players there and big Jock Govan was saying we'd take these guys no problem. Then one of the Germans, who spoke better English than Govan, told him he should not be drinking the night before a game and would be better off in his bed sleeping. Big Govan was after him in a flash but the German got away. But he was right. They gave us a good going over and after the game I remember sitting down with Bobby Combe and others and speaking about where we had gone wrong. We had been diving in and getting caught out. But it was through playing the Germans that we became more thorough and imaginative and that's how Hibs developed just through the players talking.

Brazil was something else. We stayed on the Copacabana and we could see boys playing on the beach in their bare feet. That was where their incredible control of the ball was derived from. They played at a different pace to us and we were really toiling after the flight and the humidity. In the first game against the Brazilian champions, Vasco Da Gama, we had to get a blast from oxygen masks at half-time. Subs were used in that game and I remember the boss bringing on Bill Anderson, an inside-forward who had been bought out from the Army. Bill came on as fresh as paint but after five minutes he went down and out like a light. So much for Army training compared to Hibs.

It was because Hibs were so well known abroad that we were invited into the European Cup. That's where I became the first British player to score in Europe. We gassed Rot-Weiss 4–0 although they were not a bad team with quite a few of the World Cup winning team of 1954 in their side. There was an extraordinary incident in that game when Gordon Smith let loose at the end. We thought the ref had given a fifth goal but he had blown the whistle between Gordon shooting and before it crossed the line.

I gained a wealth of experience from playing in Europe and at international level for Scotland but it still rankles today how things went wrong. We were able to go and take on Europe's best and beat them, but in Scotland this was never built on.

A lot of the blame lies with the SFA and those responsible for football at the roots. There was never enough encouragement. The Scotland set-up was all wrong. A lot of the time in those days it was a question of whether your face fitted with the selection committee. They were just a bunch of tattie merchants running a game they knew nothing about. But I have a lot of good memories. My international debut was against Belgium in 1948 just after Hibs had won the league and there were five Hibs players in the Scotland line-up: Jock Govan, Gordon Smith, Bobby Combe, Jock Shaw and me. I got another cap that season and one more against Austria in 1951 and that was it until I was called up to Scotland's World Cup campaign in 1958 and I was then 35.

I played in all of Scotland's three games and did not do badly in the 1–1 draw with Yugoslavia at half-back. I kept my eye on their brilliant winger Boskov, who went on to coach Sampdoria to the Italian title in 1991 and who is currently boss at Napoli. They were some team and their striker, Sekularac, a wee gypsy from Red Star Belgrade, was one of the best players I have played against. We lost to Paraguay and France who had Kopa and Fontaine in their side. Kopa had been brilliant against Hibs in the semi-final of the European Cup and was then with Real Madrid.

Unfortunately, my World Cup memories are a sorry story which shows how Scotland keep repeating their mistakes. It was the usual farce. Matt Busby was due to be our manager but he was incapacitated after the Munich disaster. So the tattie merchants sent us off without a manager. Dawson Scott of Clyde, the trainer, was in charge and it was the usual mess. We had a meeting and as a senior player I was asked to supervise the training.

Back home I had another season with Hibs, who were moving into a new era with players coming through like Tommy Preston, John Grant, Andy Aitken, Joe McClelland, Jackie Plenderleith, John Fraser and Joe Baker. You could see Joe was special straightaway. He was as sharp as a tack, two footed and had phenomenal pace. But I don't think Joe ever got over his car accident in Italy and was never the same player after that. Meanwhile, Hibs asked me to be trainer in 1960.

I'd asked for a free transfer and had fixed up to go to Falkirk but Hibs wouldn't let me. I would have got a few quid out of it but when Harry Swan offered me the post of trainer I went for it. But old Hugh Shaw stepped down and Walter Galbraith arrived as manager from Accrington Stanley and my ideas were totally different from his so I didn't stay too long. But the bug was there. I'd played with the best and against the best and if you did not pick up something from that it says a lot about you.

I was a great one for going abroad over the years to learn about coaching and I learned most from the Germans and the Hungarians. When I left Hibs I went to Queen's Park and when it was the English FA's centenary I was asked to coach our amateurs and we played Germany in the final at Roker Park. The great Helmut Schoen was their coach, but my side gassed them

5–2. The secretary of the German FA took a liking to me and invited me over to Germany and over the next few years I regularly went. One of the finest coaches for me was Czibor of Hungary and he produced a fantastic coaching manual. Tactically, technically and physically it was all there. The Hungarians produced great diagrams for moves which they combined with great flair and efficiency.

I always liked the challenge of out-thinking the continentals in years to come and sussing out what they were going to do. I got my first chance with Aberdeen. You hear a lot about sweepers now but 'way back in the mid-'60s I was playing Martin Buchan as a sweeper in Sofia and he was only 18 years old at the time. I built my reputation as a manager at Aberdeen and in 1971, just after winning the Cup for the second time, I got the call from Easter Road. I knew Tom Hart already as a friend and if it had been anybody but him I might not have come back to Hibs. I was a god in Aberdeen but my wife had not settled that well there so I came back.

It's not that long ago that I looked back on that team for the first time when someone gave me a video of these classic games in the early '70s.

I must admit some of it was super stuff. We started well at Hibs and in 1972 we got to the Cup final. I remember when we got through to the Station Hotel in Queen Street on the day and taking a look at them. Their faces were the colour of this page. I knew then I would have some job rustling them up for the game. Celtic were feared by everybody at that time, while Rangers were a bit of a joke. Our boys were supposed to be experienced players, but they were overawed to some degree. Well, we got slaughtered 6–1 and that could have been the end of the team. I had been in Cup finals before as player and manager so it was nothing new for me but it was for them. The only thing I could say at the time to them was that we'd be back. There followed the results of the close season and then we met them in the Drybrough Cup. It was probably a good thing meeting them so soon and right enough we gassed Celtic 5–3 and then went on to win the League Cup.

In the final we dominated the first half, then went through a rough spell with wee Jimmy Johnston turning it on, but the guys held their nerve. Big Jock Stein was some manager, but there was no love lost between us in those days. He would try and intimidate other clubs, but there was no way I was going to let him and I let him know in no uncertain terms on a couple of occasions. But these games between the two clubs has been the best football played by clubs in Scotland since the '50s.

I know that team still has a special place in Hibs supporters' hearts. People still go on to me about that team and the forwards and the midfield, but when I started the basis was the back four and keeper. For months that's all I concentrated on together with Herriot, Brownlie, Black, Blackley and Schaedler. If anything was gong to work as a unit that was the basis. That is where everything that team achieved stemmed from. I put them through all sorts of things to make sure they could handle any situation in a game.

Today I get some folk saying Jim Black was not that good individually, but I tell them to look at the 'goals against' record at that time. He was a key member and very underestimated. He was good in the air and had pace. John Blackley was a good footballer and a good supplier of the ball. Erich was a contrast to Brownlie. Strong and fast and a good tackler whereas Brownlie was a lovely player going forward. He was a full back who played like an inside-forward. He scored a lot of vital goals for us. I cannot stress enough how that team was founded on the back four. In the midfield Stanton was a good player and then there was Edwards who could put a ball on a tanner 70 yards away. His temperament let him down a lot. Cropley was a real bonus. He looked so frail but he had tremendous skill and was very hard.

So I had the back four working like a machine and the front men turning defences. I made sure Gordon and wee O'Rourke got service to the head and feet. The only one of the front five who did not score was wee Alex. He would have if he had shot more often. And then there was Arthur Duncan on the wing who had great pace but he drove me crazy at times. He was a good lad though. He had what all defenders fear – electrifying pace, but what he did with the ball at the end of it was another matter.

My philosophy at Easter Road was straightforward. Hibs' trademark had always been as a footballing side since I was there in 1946. I believed in being attack-minded and continuing that tradition. It was the Hibs way and we were famous for it.

What I tried to do as a coach was to take situations out of the game that I had come across since 1946 and show it to these 11 players. I was giving them everything I had learned since 1946 onwards. I would talk to them and if they disagreed I would say 'show me your way', but there was nothing a player could really tell me. My fate was out on the field with them.

We had some great times in Europe and the away result to Sporting Lisbon was a bit special. We lost 2–1, but it was a hell of a game in terms of tension, excitement and tactics. A board member actually had the cheek to criticise the way we played afterwards so I went straight to Hart and told him that if I had to put up with that interference I was off. The return game shut that fellow up as we won 6–1. It was tremendous stuff.

But it was another European performance in that season 1972–73 that made me think changes were needed. To be honest, I started losing interest in them after the Hadjuk Split tie. We won 4–2 at home then blew it away in Yugoslavia. They let everyone down that night. It was a close wee park, a bit like Brockville, and there was a tremendous racket and they couldn't handle it. After that I thought: they will never do it. They lost three goals from headers that I could have come out and headed away. It was disastrous. I lost faith and never regained it after that. I had thought they could have gone all the way. That was how highly I rated them. If they had kept their heads that night they could have taken anything thrown at them, but it proved too much. It was a terrible disappointment. You work like a beaver all these years and this is what happens. I knew I had made every one of them a better player. I'd made them think about the game as a team member. They were a super side but I was very disappointed. I had thought the world of the lot of them. All those hours I had spent teaching them had gone to waste. I never had the advantage of being taught like that. In my day you learned for yourself but I gave them everything I had picked up over the years.

In hindsight I may have been too hasty in breaking that side up. I brought Joe Harper in because he was the finest goal scorer in Scotland, but I think he was never accepted by the other members of the side. People forget that Jimmy O'Rourke was in the reserves and on the transfer list when I became manager. I took him off it and made him an integral part of the side. It's always up to the manager when he changes things around and professionals have to accept it. Anyway, the whole thing after Hudjuk Split turned me sour. However, there were still many fine moments and epic European struggles like the game against Leeds the next season in the UEFA Cup.

With a few new players the lads put on a tremendous show. If ever a team deserved to win it was Hibs that night at Elland Road. After the game I got a message that a Mr Johnstone would like to see me in the boardroom. I went through and who should it be but my old friend Bobby who greeted me: 'Where did you get that team, sir?' He was full of praise for the boys.

Before the game we had been training at Harrogate and I remember John Motson came out and I could see he thought it would be a walk in the park for Revie, Bremner and their Leeds team. I told him he was in for a rude awakening. And to give him his due he came back after the game and said I had been right. In the second leg Alan Gordon scored for us but Jim Black lost the ball going forward and they snapped up the chance. We lost on penalties but it was a great all-round performance.

Of all games in that era the one that lives on for most Hibs fans is the 7–0 game on New Year's Day 1973.

We had great self-belief at that time and just before the game a Hearts player contributed to their downfall by saying we were a load of cowboys. I used that on the lads. It was a foolish thing to say and Hearts suffered for it. But I did not take the same enjoyment from it the fans did. The townies are always wrapped up in the Hibs-Hearts thing but I suppose I was a foot-ball man first and foremost. Also, Hearts' manager Bobby Seith was a great friend of mine. We had gone on coaching courses together at Largs so what could I say to him after the game. He was feeling sick. But saying that it was some performance and I enjoyed watching a video of it that my son-in-law gave me.

Of course Hibs continued to be a force to be reckoned with challenging for the league, qualifying for Europe and there was the three-game Cup final in 1979. We were robbed in the first game when McCloy crucified Campbell in the box near the end and that would have given us the Cup. I had no complaints about referees early in my career when I thought some of them were great, but latterly as a player and as a manager I saw a fair amount of bias towards Rangers. Both as a player and a mana-ger I liked playing Rangers and we usually gave them a good going over. They got results with Jock Wallace as manager but they were never a football team. That 1979 team had some good boys. Jackie McNamara was a good servant to Hibs and a great tackler. He did it just like they did in the old days. I liked big

George Stewart. He was a lovely lad and Hibs daft like wee Jimmy O'Rourke. Ally McLeod up front was something else. People said he was lazy, but he had more of a football brain in his pinkie than most other players had in their whole body.

And then there was George Best who came just after that. George was a complete footballer. He had so much vision and at his peak he had complete skill, pace, two feet, superb dribbling and he could shoot, head and tackle. He had the whole lot. It was Tom Hart's idea to go for him and we knew he was well past it but in every game he was still too many moves ahead of the rest. He was a lovely guy, Georgie boy, and he used to come back in the afternoon and was brilliant with the young boys. But Best was Best and if he was up in the hotel on the drink what could you do about it? He was his own man.

Other members of that team don't get the credit they deserve. Des Bremner was some player and he went on to win a European Cup medal with Aston Villa. You could count on him to win the ball, give it to one of his own players, then he'd win it back again for us and lay it off to one of our own.

Another player was Ally Brazil. He took some stick from the crowd and whenever he made a mistake they would crucify him. But ask players who played with him. He was a players' player and they appreciated what he was doing and I wasn't the only manager that kept picking him.

By the time I gave up managing Hibs the disillusionment with Scottish football had really set in. The Premier League killed everything. It's ridiculous playing each other four times. There's no middle in the league now, just a top and bottom and teams are frightened to bring through young players. I thought the game was going downhill in Scotland anyway and you only need to look around nowadays at the lack of fluency, organisation and flair. All the players are interested in are dibs, dibs and dibs. I have always thought players did not work hard enough at the game in Scotland as the European players did. Even the English are superior to Scottish teams. You still see Scottish teams kick off, pass back and then hump it up the park. Have they not learned that nine-tenths of the game is possession?

Of the current Hibs team I like the look of Kevin Harper. He has lightning pace, but the boy must be brought on so he learns to exploit his pace at the right time. Michael O'Neill is a clever player and can make them tick and he plays like a real inside-forward. But saying all that I would still love to be out there as a player or coach. I loved every minute. There is one guy who I learned a lot from who nobody now remembers, David Russell who was in East Fife's 1938 Cup-winning team.

Looking back I know I had a reputation for being tough, maybe too tough, but I was always doing it for the players' benefit. I was demanding perfection because if you are going to do a job you must do it to the best of your ability. I was a great one for discipline. I learned that in the Navy and what an asset it was to me. If you lose your discipline on the field you will lose the game.

My pride in Hibs was evident in all details about the club and that's why I changed Hibs back to their traditional strip when I took over as manager. I always thought we had the smartest strip in Britain without a shadow of a doubt. These green shirts, white sleeves and green socks with white tops were something special. As a player everything was perfectly prepared. Each Friday the trainer, Jimmy McColl, would hang the strips on their pegs and the wee chairman would come down to inspect every jersey, jockstrap, the lot. Everything had to be perfect. And the first thing I did when I took over as manager was throw the training gear in the rubbish bin and got a brand new lot from Thornton's. And with Tom McNiven I would hang up the strips. I was brought up that way. I wanted Hibs to go out looking the best as it would make the players feel good and the fans proud of them.

As for the famous old story about Eddie and Alan Gordon when he told the university-educated striker after one interruption too many at a tactics talk: 'The trouble with you, Gordon, is aw yer brains are in yer fuckin' heid.' All Eddie will say is: 'Aye, and so they were.'

Xile
CLOTHING
Est 1984

KICK OFF
THE SEASON
WITH XILE

INTEREST FREE CREDIT
NOW AVAILABLE AT
XILE

CHAPTER FOUR

ROCK 'N' ROLL FOOTBALLER

Nowadays we live in an age of hype. Players, performances, managers and goals are blown out of all proportion. Sensationalism is the name of the game. Yet they were different times when a teenager exploded on the Scottish football scene in the late '50s. The media then was far more restrained and balanced. But the impact he made was incredible and the coverage he got was more in keeping with today's hypomania.

Even the *Scotsman*, which was then the epitome of a conservative and somewhat dour newspaper, was taken to task for filling too many column inches about the amazing feats of the Baker Boy. But they could be excused because Joseph Baker really was a sensation.

The dynamic boy wonder scored 159 goals in four seasons with Hibs. As well as his talent he had that special, indefinable quality that makes a star. Just as Best and Charlton were magnificent players at Manchester United, it was Denis Law the United fans called 'The King'. At Easter Road while the Famous Five were revered, Joe Baker was the fans' golden boy. Part of it was surely to do with his youth and his style of play. He was the first post-war star. The Famous Five bore the hallmark of another era – the war, austerity, short back 'n' sides, national service etc – but Joe was your first rock 'n' roll footballer. Elvis may have been king, but Hibs had the Baker Boy.

Despite his distinguished football career which saw him play for Torino in Italy, capped for England and star with Arsenal and Nottingham Forrest as well as Sunderland, his days with Hibs were the best years of his football life.

To me Hibs is my first love. I can never forget my times at Easter Road and the fans who have always been tremendous to me. It amazes me even today the way they still treat me when I come to Easter Road. I cannot really find the words to express how I felt when they arranged the testimonial dinner a couple of years ago. That night I turned up at the Hibs Supporters Club I had a speech prepared, but my bottle went when I went in and saw the packed tables and the reception they gave me. I was so overcome with emotion that I could just barely say thank you and sit down. It was great to see so many of my former teammates there, but I would really have needed three days to properly talk to them all.

At the do at the Sheraton I hope I showed people how I feel about the club when I presented them with two of my caps. They must be unique as they come from two different countries. I don't know how many players have achieved that. But one was a Scottish schoolboys cap and the other one of my England caps. I said that night I did not consider they were leaving my family as I considered Hibs part of my family.

What is hard to believe is Joe's claim he was not really all that interested in football.

It was brother Gerry who played for Hibs after me that really got me into it. I was born in Liverpool during the war as my father was in the Navy but the family returned to Scotland six weeks after I was born. Gerry had been born earlier on the family travels in New York. This twist of fate was to have long term consequences that no one foresaw but which I have always deeply regretted. Although Gerry and I grew up in deepest Lanarkshire we would never be able to play for Scotland. Nowadays it would be no problem when you look at guys like Andy Goram and Stuart McCall with their Coronation Street accents. But the rules didn't change till 1967. So it was too late for me to be eligible for Scotland.

Growing up as a lad I was encouraged by my brother Gerry who played boys club football. As a schoolboy I scored five for Lanarkshire against Edinburgh at Tynecastle which I suppose was an omen of things to come. That ground was always a happy hunting ground for me. When Gerry was offered terms by Chelsea I was only 15 but went down with him to keep him company.

In a trial game Chelsea were short of a man so Gerry told Ted Rae, Chelsea manager, that I could play and so I did and scored four goals. They offered me S forms, but after six weeks I had had enough of London and returned home. But Hibs scout

Davie Wyper brought me under his wing and he did the best thing possible to influence me. He invited me to Easter Road for the semi-final of the European Cup against Reims.

Of course I was wanting Hibs to win that night, but I could not keep my eyes off Raymond Kopa. He was a fantastic player and that along with the tremendous atmosphere really convinced me I wanted to be a professional. I always loved the big crowds and that is often the difference if a good young player can make it or not. If he thrives on that pressure he is half way there already.

I was then farmed out to Armadale Thistle where I teamed up with Johnny MacLeod who was to star with me at senior level not only at Easter Road but also at Highbury.

It was in the 1957/58 season that I made my debut as a 17-year-old against Airdrie. I well remember the rough reception to senior football as we lost 4–1 and big Doug Baillie bounced me round Broomfield.

The next game I played was to mark the opening of Hearts' floodlights at Tynecastle and I scored one of Hibs' four goals. Then we played Queens Park and I scored two and everything seemed to snowball from there. I loved my football so much that a game could have lasted two days and I would have still been running. I suppose people kept waiting for the bubble to burst, but it just seemed to grow and grow. Straight away the Hibs fans took to me which is important for a young lad and the support they gave me was tremendous. Their encouragement was superb and it really brought my career on more than I did.

At the time there was a midweek floodlit league with English clubs and I made a mark in a few of them. I rattled in a hat-trick against Tottenham Hotspur and got another against Wolves who were a top club at that time. I was up against England captain Billy Wright and did not badly, scoring three as we won 5–2. I was zipping past him at such a speed his shorts were on fire.

Goals just seemed to keep coming and I got another hat trick in the league against St Mirren. I was making a name for myself but what really did it with the Hibs fans was when we met Hearts that season in the third round of the Cup. Hearts were racing away to win the league that season and no one gave us a chance, but it remains one of my most memorable games for Hibs. The whole city was at fever pitch and Hearts went ahead, but I scored two before Hearts equalised. Then I banged in another couple and the eventual score was 4–3. Pace was always one of my greatest assets and at that age I would run forever and poor old Jimmy Milne, the Hearts centre half, got a right roasting that day.

I was lucky to have experienced players alongside me. At times Lawrie Reilly was inside right although he was carrying an injury and in the Hearts game 'The Duke', John Grant, was riding shotgun. I scored another in the quarter-finals against Third Lanark and then it was Rangers in the semis with us squeezing through 2–1 in a replay.

In hindsight I can say I should not have played in the final. I do not think manager Hugh Shaw realised I was burnt out and exhausted. I was still only 17 and overawed by the occasion. Today they are far more careful how youngsters are brought on. Anyway the whole occasion got to me a bit. Mind you it would have been a brave man who left me out, such was the clamour from the fans at the time, but in hindsight I reckon they would have done better without me.

However Joe had scored 29 goals in 45 games, in that his first season.

I started the next season with a hat-trick of headers against Aberdeen and it was then that I got a call-up to the England Under-23 squad to play against Poland with a couple of nippers called Bobby Charlton and Jimmy Greaves as inside forwards. I was to go on and win eight full England caps as well as four Under-23 caps.

I could not believe it at first when England called me up. I even laughed about it. I did not feel English at all and have always felt a bit sick that I never got a chance to play for Scotland. However the rules at that time were strictly you played for your country of birth. My brother Gerry even ended up playing for America, his country of birth. I have always wondered why they wanted me. They had Charlton and Greaves, Brian Clough, Bobby Smith and Geoff Hurst over the years when I played. But they wanted me and that was that and I became the first player outside the Football League to play for England.

My first full cap came against Ireland in November 1959. I also took some stick down south. Desmond Hackett in the *Daily Express* asked 'Why bring a Scotsman to play for England?' But it did not get me down and after 25 minutes I scored with a 25-yard shot. Within half an hour after the game I was on a plane back to Scotland. The press wondered where I was and called me the ghost on account of my quick getaway. I never really settled with the England squad and in some ways felt I was never really accepted. I also think that the England squads, despite the great players they have, have less team spirit than Scottish squads.There was also the occasion in the taxi from the airport that put me off playing for England. When I jumped in and told the cabbie I wanted the England training camp he gave me a funny look. He started chatting away asking why I wanted to go there. When I told him I was playing for England he gave me a funny look and went quiet. I didn't pay much attention as he was whispering away on his radio but the next thing I knew we were pulling over and a police car came alongside. The boy was out the taxi in a flash shouting to the cops 'That's him there, in the back'. You'd have thought I was public enemy number one. The guy had thought I was some mad Scotsman and who knows what I would do when I got to the England camp, but a phone call to Walter Winterbottom cleared things up.

I got 25 league goals in season 1958/59 and another five in other competitions. The next season I scored 42 league goals as Hibs netted 106 times in all, more than that season's champions, Hearts. However, the following season was to be my last at Easter Road when I scored a total of 44 goals.

Games that stand out were when I scored four against Airdrie in the League Cup and five against Third Lanark in the league and, of course, the nine against Peebles Rovers in the Cup. The funny thing is I hardly remember anything about the Peebles Rovers game. And that's not the passage of time. Straight after the game I could hardly remember a thing. Every time I got the ball the goal just seemed to be opening up in front of me. But I suppose it is the performances in the Inter Cities Fairs Cup against Barcelona and Roma which sealed my fate.

Barcelona had just knocked Real Madrid out of the European Cup and were desperate to go one better than Real by entering and winning two European competitions. We were due to play them a couple of weeks before Christmas but heavy fog wiped the game out so the first leg was switched to Barcelona on 27 December. We set out on Boxing Day in good spirits as we'd beaten Third Lanark 8–4 on the Saturday and I'd equalled the club record of five goals in one game held by Gordon Smith.

Manager Hughie Shaw changed our tactics so we were not chasing the game. Sammy Baird and John Grant were making sure the boys weren't jumping into tackles and holding off and playing the Spaniards at their own game. Meanwhile I was told to chase every ball and run their defenders as hard as I could. I scored after ten minutes when I followed up on a ball the goalkeeper couldn't hold and then Johnny MacLeod scored a beauty. Their Hungarian star Koscis pulled one back before half-time and I hit the post just on the whistle. They equalised again but the defence was superb with Jim Easton, just a youngster at the time, outstanding. As we soaked up pressure we hit them on the counter attack with ten minutes to go when Tam Preston hammered in one to make it 3–2. Straight away from the kick-off we won possession as they were too eager and I was released and raced off to make it four. It was some finish as they pulled two back with Koscis getting his hat trick. The Nou Camp was in pandemonium and the crowd gave us an ovation. It was a shock result and it made Europe sit up and take notice but I didn't realise they were looking at me.

But still the press did not give us a chance back home as Barcelona had taken over from Real Madrid as Europe's top team. The whole of Edinburgh was hyped up for the second leg. It was an electrifying occasion and I scored early on, gliding in a header from Johnny MacLeod's free kick. Barcelona equalised and then Koscis put them ahead. We piled on the pressure and they started to use heavy tactics and twice I was decked in the box. It was Tommy Preston who drew us level, heading in a Willie Ormond corner that had been knocked on by Sammy Baird. There were over 50,000 in Easter Road and they were roaring us on. I put Johnny MacLeod free in the penalty box and he was pulled down with five minutes to go. There was mayhem as their keeper attacked the ref. His team-mates restrained him and Bobby Kinloch had been waiting all this time and coolly scored. That's when it really started. You had to be there to believe it. The Barcelona players chased the referee up to the centre circle and the police had to come on to protect him. The game restarted after about seven minutes and the last five were mayhem as they kicked at everything that moved. The referee spent the whole time on the touchline by the tunnel waiting to blow and take off as fast as he could. Not so lucky was the far side linesman whom Barcelona decided to take it out on instead. But the Hibs players and police helped him get inside. But that wasn't the end of it as a few of the Barcelona players tried to kick in the referees' door. Barcelona had gone totally crazy and they should have gone to jail for what they got up to that night.

In the semi-final we played Roma, but were sold down the river by Harry Swan and the board at the time. Both games were draws so we needed a replay. The Hibs board wanted to make more money out of getting half the gate receipts from a game in Rome rather than the advantage of playing at home or on a neutral ground. Remember it was the semi-final of a European competition. I scored two in the first game at Easter Road that finished in a draw. When we arrived in Rome for the second leg there was a heatwave, but come the afternoon of the game the heavens opened up and lightning zig-zagged across the sky. Eddie Turnbull pulled a stroke getting Bobby Kinloch to switch jerseys with me and the Italians didn't twig until we were 3–1 ahead. Poor old Bobby though had to take a lot of stick that was meant for me. But Bobby equalised after they went ahead and then I scored two. They were a good team and pulled two back to draw. What happened next I'll never understand. The third game play-off was to be played in Rome a month later.

But the writing was on the wall as far as my staying with Hibs. The board had already decided to sell me. I did not want to leave and it is interesting to think what would have happened if I could have spent my whole career at Hibs. I really enjoyed playing for Hibs fans although to be truthful it was not all that good a team we had. However I always wonder how many goals I could have scored for the club if I had stayed.

I was on a wage of £12 at the time and all I asked for was a £5 pay rise. I'd spoken to some of the senior pros about it like Willie Ormond. I didn't think it was too much to ask, but the next thing I knew it was in the papers and Hibs were open to offers. The board had already set me up in a deal with the Italians. So they used this as an excuse saying they could not meet my demands as the supporters would think I was asking for the world. But as I've said it was only a fiver on top of the £12 a week I was earning. I did not want to go and no newspaper asked me for my side of the story at the time. I was still just a kid and did not know how to handle that kind of thing.

The Italian agent Gigi Peronace appeared in Edinburgh and I knew they wanted me and Denis Law. So there were rumours and comings and goings in the lead up to the semi-finals with Italian agents in and out of Edinburgh. It was hardly the best way to prepare for the semi-final. When I went to Italy for the second leg it was like the Keystone Cops with agents and reporters chasing around between the hotel, airport and training ground. The fact I scored in both games only increased the interest of the Italians.

Meanwhile Hibs were getting half the receipts and travel costs paid for in the third game. Worse was to follow as we had to wait a month for the game. The Scottish league was complete so we had to wait for Roma finishing their league campaign. That long lay-off had a big effect on the outcome as we went to Rome short of match practice. It was to prove to be my last game for Hibs at that stage of my career and it was a terrible way to finish. We ended up beaten 6–0 and I was on my way to Italy.

Everything would have been great in Italy if only I did not have to play football. *Catenaccio* – their style of defensive football – was at its height and there was so much kicking, elbowing, fingers in the eyes, spitting etc. Jimmy Greaves had only lasted four months with AC Milan. I was sharing a house with Denis Law and neither of us settled. I came back from training one day and Denis was offski. He never said a word. Just took off, clearing out our wardrobes. Whenever I've seen him since then I always say : 'Denis, what about those five suits you took, they were mine'.

Italian football is totally different nowadays. It's tremendous stuff with so many goals. I just wonder how Joe Baker and Denis Law would have done in today's league. We would have been greased lightning and scored a multitude. But when I was there it was all downhill after the car accident. The club gave me an Alfa-Romeo sports car which went like a racehorse. Denis suggested we took it out late one night for a spin when the roads were quiet. All I remember is trying to slow down approaching a roundabout. The next thing I knew I was waking up in hospital two weeks later. I was very fortunate and they did five operations on me before I woke up. The wife said they did a good job although they forgot to put the brain back in!

So when the Arsenal offer came along I was delighted to take it and scored over 100 goals for them in four seasons before moving on to Nottingham Forest. The first season there they were nearly relegated, but the next year we were pipped by a point for the league by Manchester United and knocked out of the FA Cup semi-finals 2–1 by Spurs. There followed a not-so-happy spell at Sunderland until 1971. After a game I was told there was somebody to see me. It turned out to be Tom Hart and Dave Ewing, Hibs manager at the time.

They wanted me back at Hibs. The idea of going back had never occurred to me but it was a very emotional reunion. The reception I got when I ran out the tunnel made me realise what I had been missing all these years. I capped it all with a goal along with Pat Stanton as we brought Aberdeen's winning run of 15 games in a row to a halt. It could have been two as I had another goal disallowed. Hibs had won for the first time in 10 games and although I joined with less than a third of the season to go I finished top scorer with eight goals.

In the close season Eddie Turnbull took over as Hibs manager. Meanwhile I'd picked up a nasty injury which finished my career with Hibs. It led to calcification of the calf muscle. I was coming on 32 and I feel Eddie Turnbull did not give me a chance to recover. It was no secret that there was no love lost between Eddie and me and it didn't surprise me I didn't fit into his plans. Eddie was a great player and somebody I learned a lot from playing beside at the beginning of my career, but as trainer he overdid it and often left the players washed out. But I can understand it as the surgeon at one point said there was no chance of my coming back. Football is like that and you soon learn it is a bit of a rat race. But I look back on it and the good times. The thing that stands out is the way Hibs supporters were good to me in those days and still are today.

CHAPTER FIVE

THE REBEL

It would have been a travesty if the rebel had never played for Hibs, but it was a close-run thing. While '50s teenagers worshipped Jimmy Dean, Hibs fans took to a rebel with a cause. It was the Bonnyrigg boy Eric Stevenson who turned his back on a place at Tynecastle to cross the city to the team he loved. Forever after that Hibs fans had a special affection for Stevie, a dazzling winger who joined Hibs at the end of the '50s and helped them to swing through the '60s.

Pat Stanton's fond of saying 'You'll never meet a winger with a brain in his heid', but he will always make an exception for Eric Stevenson. 'Eric always knew what he was doing on the park. He was some player.'

Eric was brought up in a Hibs-daft family and his uncle Tam Clark was the chairman of Bonnyrigg Hibs supporters club and took the Young Stevie to see the Famous Five.

As a lad Eric played with Edina Hearts alongside John Greig and Chris Shevlane.

There were about 14 of us on Hearts books as Davie Johnstone who ran the club, was a former Hearts player. So I went on S forms as a 15-year-old when I left school and went down the pits. Meanwhile I trained a couple of nights a week at Tynecastle and played in a few reserve games and one of them was against Hibs.

When I turned 17 a few English clubs came after me, among them Manchester United and Wolves. Jimmy Murphy, Matt Busby's assistant, came up to the house and invited me down to Old Trafford. I also went to see Wolverhampton. When I came back I found out I was registered as a Hearts player which was news to me as I was sure I was only on S forms. So I went to Davie Johnstone and asked him what was up as I had only ever signed an S form. Davey said I must have signed for the club full-time otherwise I couldn't be registered. Anyway something was wrong and word soon spread. Sure enough George Smith, the Hibs scout, appeared at the door. He told me the way to get out of it all was to sign for Hibs. A lot was happening behind the scenes and Hibs were pretty sharp off the mark. My uncle was desperate for me to sign with Hibs and so was I. What Hearts had done was strictly illegal and it gave me a way out. Anyway the outcome was I signed for Hibs. Meanwhile Hearts and their manager Tommy Walker were fined by the SFA. They had been paying me £3 a week which I had paid into a bank so I had to give it back to Hearts. But I was glad it was all behind me and only too delighted to get the chance to play for my team.

At the start of 1959/60 season I arrived at Easter Road. And what a life it was for me stepping out of the pits and going full-time with Hibs. I loved every minute of it and was always first in to training. It was just great training with the likes of Joe Baker, Johnny MacLeod, Tam Preston and Bobby Johnstone who had come back to Hibs after his spell down south. Eddie Turnbull, who had stepped up to take over as trainer, took an instant shine to me. Years later, whenever I was up playing against Aberdeen, Ned would take me aside and tell me he had tried to sign me but Hibs had refused. I think he tried on about three occasions.

It didn't take me long to appreciate Eddie's know-how. I remember in an early practice game Eddie played at right half and he gave me a lot of guidance. It was then I realised his great vision for the game. I know everyone speaks about Smith, Johnstone, Ormond and Reilly but Turnbull was streets ahead of them in reading the game. When it came to a football brain he was head and shoulders above not only them but anybody else you care to mention.

As a Hibs supporter I loved hearing the bootroom banter and stories of the Famous Five first hand. Lawrie Reilly was my hero. I remember going into Tam Preston's pub the Traveller's Tryst at the bus station and John Paterson told me I was the only player of the current lot who would get into their team. It was a brilliant compliment. Anyway he took me to meet Reilly and I was like a wee boy in front of my hero. Tam would tell us stories about Lawrie and how he would go boxing in training if he was getting beaten and squared up to big Tommy Younger on a few occasions. Lawrie was a big headed so-and-so and the lads like to tell of the time they were in McVitie's at the West End, a regular haunt in those days. Some guy who obviously wasn't a big fan of Lawrie's piped up as they came in 'Hey Reilly, I see the Hibs beat the Hearts without you on Saturday.' Lawrie turned round and said 'Do you know where I was on Saturday – at Wembley in front of 100,000 and I scored the winning goal. That shows you how good I am.' He was never shy, was Lawrie. I loved watching him and the way he threw himself about and got in there especially against the likes of George Young and Willie Woodburn. Lawrie was always in the thick of things and really exciting to watch.

During the years ahead at Hibs there were some superb performances but also a lot of inconsistency. Hibs played in cavalier style with many class players, but the game was changing and our approach was often a touch old fashioned compared to the more tactically astute and defensive sides. Ironically enough I left Hibs just when my old mentor Eddie Turnbull returned as manager in 1971. What Eddie did was to combine Hibs flair with tactical savvy and organisation.

I went to Ayr and had been there about six months when I met Pat Stanton and he told me I wouldn't recognise the old place. In his opinion the fun had gone out the game when Eddie arrived. But to be honest Easter Road was a bit too much like a holiday camp in the '60s. We had a great time and I am sure the fans loved a lot of it, but the fun in general was going out of football. Turnbull was of the modern era and realised you needed to have a thoroughly professional approach or you would never win anything.

It's a fact of modern life but I would still prefer to see skill and adventure and I think most Hibs fans are like that. I am still a regular at Easter Road and I would prefer Hibs to lose 5–4 than draw 0–0. Take a player like Mickey Weir – I would have him in the team every week. It's great what he can do with a ball and that's what the fans want. But maybe the manager wants him to cover back etc. Fair enough, the manager's judged on results and has to get them as he sees fit. Today a more modern player is a guy like Keith Wright who is a great worker but to be quite frank he could not lace Joe Baker's boots, just like the rest of the strikers in the Premier Division. But he is the type of player most managers want these days rather than your Mickey Weirs.

Then there was the boy Hamilton who couldn't string three passes together yet could run all day – another modern player.

There are another couple who got into the first team but would not have got in the third team when I was a player. That shows you the state of the game today.

If Joe Baker was around today I reckon he would be worth £9 million. One of my first games was as inside forward alongside Joe. Can you imagine how I felt? The season I joined he scored 42 goals. He was some guy Joe and he never changed. He was still the same when he came back in 1970. He was a lively guy and suited to the times. People forget what a mark Joe made. I remember we were down at Longniddry training and you should have seen the crowd that gathered and all these girls were mobbing him, wanting his autograph. I have to admit he was a good-looking bugger in those days. I had not been there long when we went down to Queen of the South and Joe ordered a coffee in the hotel after our pre-match meal. He said 'Stevie, do you want one'. The waiter brought two over and I just about choked as I had a sip. I don't know how many brandies were in it. Joe just said 'You must have mine', snatched it over and downed the lot. And this was before the game. What's more he went out and banged in a couple of goals.

The sad thing was that Joe's last season was my first. He was brilliant against Barcelona, especially the away game when he scored two and even Ned said he thought it was Hibs' finest performance. In the semi-final he scored twice away to Roma and the play-off was his last game for the club. That was in Rome and the less said about how that happened, the better. But Harry Swan told us to enjoy a wee holiday; we had earned it on the toss of the coin. It was a good few weeks after the season had ended. I played in that game and we lost 6–0. But still it was a great experience and I remember their Uruguayan, Schiaffino. What a player he was, even if he was about 50. During that time the Italian agent Gigi Peronace was hanging around Joe. He always had a glass in his hand. Mind you, so did Joe. He was always taking the mickey out of Gigi and I think the only Italian Joe ever picked up was 'money, money'. I really don't think the Italians knew what they were taking on when they signed Joe and Denis Law – a right couple of comedians.

When Joe returned in 1970 we went on a pre-season tour to Majorca. It was really a holiday with a couple of games thrown in. Just about the first day Joe, my room-mate, got me up saying: 'Come on, we are going for a walk. We need some exercise'. Well, we must have done a tour of all the British bars in the resort and every bar had yon song 'Chirpy Chirpy, Cheep, Cheep' blaring away. As we got back to the hotel all the rest of lads could hear was 'Chirpy, Chirpy, Cheep Cheep' coming up the drive and Joe and me dancing our way in. That night we played and drew 2–2 with Joe and me scoring. The chairman Tom Hart came bursting in and started slagging the younger lads. 'You should be ashamed of yourself. We should have won and only got a result thanks to these two. Let them be an example. That's what dedication does for you.'

There were a lot of special players around then that have been forgotten. One was Davie Gibson and no disrespect to current players, but he was streets ahead of any of them. I always prided myself on a bit of vision and knew how and when to play a one-two. Davey was a master at it. He was so good he would not have been out of place alongside Cantona. But he was transferred to Leicester City by Walter Galbraith in 1962.

Another one who stood out was Willie Hamilton. He was something else. I have met some crazy men in my time, but none like Willie. The problem with Willie though was he would only play every six games and then that would only be for ten minutes. But mind you it was some 10 minutes. The only man who could get him to do anything was big Jock Stein and Willie had some superb games with Stein. When we played Real Madrid Willie outshone the likes of Puskas and that season we did the treble over Rangers. Willie was outstanding showing the likes of Jim Baxter up. But like I said he was some man.

There's the famous story of him and the silver salver in Canada. We had gone over for a tournament and each team represented a city and we were playing for Toronto. Bob Shankly had told Neil Martin, Willie and me that if we won one game we did not have to play in the next. So we arrived in Ottawa after a win and had a few bevvies. Then a taxi driver asked us which one was going to win the silver salver. It was the first we had heard about this Man of the Match award.

At the stadium the three of us went out and took off our blazers to do a bit of sunbathing. It was about 100 degrees and Willie was sweating like a pig. We dozed off and then the next thing we knew the game was due to start. Willie had vanished and Neilie and me were wondering where he had gone. The next thing I know is big Neilie's nudging me. 'Do you see what I see?' Willie had nipped in and got changed. He had grabbed a place in the team as he obviously thought the silver salver would be worth a bob or two. Well, what a game he had. He scored seven and was pushing folk out the way to get to the ball and shooting from 70 yards. Sure enough he got his salver and most folk have heard how he bent it in two to squeeze it into his holdall the next day as we were leaving.

People still go on about a goal he scored from an impossible angle against Hearts on New Year's Day. The night before we had stayed in the Scotia Hotel so the management could keep an eye on us. Come midnight the champagne was brought in but none of the players would take any and were off to bed; bar Willie that is. At about four in the morning Tam McNiven hears banging on his door. It's Willie wanting someone to have a drink with him. He'd scoffed the lot of the champagne down the stairs. He was looking rough the next day, but what a screamer of a goal he scored from an impossible angle out on the byeline. But that was enough for us and for him. He didn't do another thing as we comfortably held on to win 1–0.

I had fond memories of playing against Hearts and a special game was the 4–0 win in 1966 at Tynecastle. Jimmy O'Rourke had been out the team but got his chance because Neil Martin was injured and both of us scored twice in the first 10 minutes. I always loved playing against Hearts and I can assure you we regularly beat them in those days. After going four up we were content to take the piss. Nowadays the coaches would be off the bench to keep you going forward but we had done the business. I suppose we could have gone on and got more than seven that day. Maybe even nine, but we didn't have that target to aim at as that game was a few years away.

I felt I was always appreciated as a flair player by the fans from my debut in 1960. Also making their debuts that day were Sammy Baird and Ronnie Simpson. Sammy had come from Rangers and Ronnie from Newcastle but we lost 2–0 against St Johnstone. We then played a friendly at Swansea on the following Monday, winning 4–2 and I got one. However, the next game brought me back down to earth. We got hammered 6–0 by Celtic at home and I never got a kick at the ball. But it was the next season I really established myself. Willie Ormond who was at the end of his days as a player was injured so I played on the left wing against Celtic in the Cup. We drew 1–1 and I was up against Duncan Mackay who'd been capped for Scotland. In the replay John Clark scored within two minutes. It was some night as the Celtic fans broke into the graveyard and knocked over gravestones. But from then on I stayed on the left wing and when Willie Ormond came back he played at left half.

Wee Willie was great to me and never resented me coming into his place. He looked after me when I first joined. One time we were down at North Berwick and he and Tam Preston took me for a drink. 'What do you wan?'t Willie asked. 'Same as you.' It was a big mistake. They were on the G&Ts and I was sick as a pig later. When we went to Barcelona on our first big foreign trip Willie told Jim Scott and me to stick with him. That was the sort of guy he was, looking after the young laddies.

It was hardly surprising Hibs dipped after selling Joe to Torino and also with the likes of Willie Ormond and Davie Gibson moving on. Johnny MacLeod was also off to Arsenal where he teamed up with Joe a season later.

Hugh Shaw resigned as manager early in the next season and Walter Galbraith was brought in as manager. He'd played at full back for Queens Park, Clyde and Grimsby and had managed Accrington Stanley, Bradford PA and Tranmere Rovers. We knew Galbraith was not the solution. A lot of us thought Hibs should have put Ned in the job. But the boy they got was unbelieveable. Walter Galbraith was the spitting image of Douglas Fairbanks and you could tell he thought so too. He'd come into the dressing-room and say 'everything okay?' and that was the team talk. The mirror was right by the door and he'd always stop and look in the mirror, check himself out and away he went. I remember in 1961 he organised a tour to Czechoslovakia and everyone turned up at the airport bar the manager. No one knew where he was. So finally someone phoned him at home and we were told he was in bed with the flu. He had never thought to tell anyone. So we got on the plane without him and Ned was in charge.

Bang went any chance of a holiday. There were 10 p.m. curfews each night and no one was allowed to drink. Ned was some man and after our third game we were sitting out up in the mountains. We were seven days in with a couple of wins under our belts and thought even Ned might think it was time to relax.

Somebody asked if Ned would drop the curfew and let us drink. Not too surprisingly he refused so John Fraser said 'Well I'll be getting away to my bed boys, goodnight boss' and started to head off. Ned growled 'You sit on yir fucking arse. You'll go to bed when I tell you to go.'

Needless to say, back home Galbraith's days were numbered and a new era dawned as Jock Stein came from Dunfermline at the start of season 1964/65. One of the first things Jock Stein did was move Pat Stanton who had come in 1963 as an inside forward from Bonnyrigg to sweeper. If they had left Pat at sweeper I'm sure he would still be playing yet. But Sloop (John Blackley) was to come along and that was the only position he could play so Pat went to right half. However Pat would have established himself as the best sweeper in Britain if he had been allowed to play there. I'm sure he would also have won umpteen caps for Scotland in that role. Don't get me wrong, Pat was some right half. He could tackle, score, was better than most in the air and read the game well. At the back he was like Willie Miller but better. He was never a shouter, he just played his game.

However when Jock went Pat was moved up again. I remember when Bob Shankly resigned we were without a manager for a while. So one of the directors told Tam McNiven to pick the team. Now Tam was a great physio and really good guy, but he couldnae spell 'football' let alone pick the team. So the senior players got together and ran the team for a few games.

Sloop wanted to play in the middle of the park so he did in the first game. But after 20 minutes it was obvious he hadn't a clue so I said, 'Pat you'll have to move back into midfield.' But the funny thing was we did well without a manager and won a few games before Willie McFarlane was appointed.

During the Jock Stein era I took part in some outstanding games, such as a 2–0 defeat of Real Madrid and the treble over Rangers. We were some team at the time with Pat, Peter Cormack, Pat Quinn, Neil Martin and Willie Hamilton.

We got off to a good start as well winning the Summer Cup against Aberdeen. I scored what I thought was the winner in extra time in the second leg at Easter Road but Charlie Cooke lobbed in an equaliser. But we beat them well in the play-off 3–1. I often played well against Aberdeen and I remember one time in the League Cup we drew up in Aberdeen 1–1 and Ned had George Murray marking me. I hardly got a kick and Ned told me later what happened before the second leg was a lesson to him. George Murray said he could take care of me and play his own game going forward. The surprising thing was that Ned listened, as he usually listened to no one. Anyway, I had a stormer, scoring a couple and laying on the others. I had to go off in the second half because I could hardly breathe. I'm sure that was the last time Ned listened to any players.

Part of life in the '60s at Easter Road consisted of classic continental clashes with huge crowds. The game every one speaks about was the Napoli one and it was something else but there were other great clashes such as the Leeds tie when we went out due to the four-step rule. Colin Stein had put us ahead when Willie Wilson got caught out going round Mick Jones. From the free kick Jack Charlton scored. Another cracker was the Hamburg game. Away goals had just been introduced and we went out after winning 2–1 at home. They were a good team and had Uwe Seeler playing and the World Cup centre half Willie Schulz. They were kicking everything that moved that night and we must have had about 50 corners. We even got a penalty and Joe Davis of all people missed it. He was usually a certainty from the spot.

Travelling abroad with Hibs had its lighter moments especially if guys like Willie Hamilton and Joe Baker were along for the trip. It was always a time for pulling one over your mates, such as the time in Canada when a few of the more inexperienced travellers were caught out by room service. Jim Scott and I shared a room but we knew anything on room service got docked from our pocket money. So one night we suggested to Billy Simpson and Allan McGraw that we order up some T-bone steaks and a few beers from their room. Big John McNamee was there and he was all for it. We had a good nosh up and a good few beers. So a night or so later Big John invites us to his room for another slap-up. A couple of days later Tam McNiven's handing out spending money: 'Stevenson $80, Scott $80, McGraw, Simpson and McNamee . . . you owe us $50. You should have seen their faces, but you did not hang around if Big John was narked.

On another occasion Hibs went to play Bellenenses in Portugal after drawing 3–3 at Easter Road. It was 0–0 at half time and as I came off Ned started giving me a right bollocking, 'What the fuck are you playing at, yer fucking useless'. I was only 18 so I was a bit sensitive. I went out and scored a goal in the second half and we were on our way to a 3–1 win.

I was in the huff with him after the game and kept away from him. Afterwards me and Scottie passed Ned, Sammy Baird and 'The Duke', John Grant, having a drink. Scottie says 'Hey

Eddie, you're no shouting at him now'. Ned turned on us: 'If these two bastards weren't here now I'd batter the pair of you'. His dander was up that night and that wasn't the end of it. Back at the hotel we heard a commotion and looked out the window. A taxi had pulled up with Ned, Sammy and 'The Duke' in the back seat. Ned wasn't paying for it and Sammy was sure he wasn't either. So he bolted out his door followed by 'The Duke' as Ned tried to get out the other side but it was locked. All we could hear was the taxi driver shouting 'Money, you give me money'. Ned was having none of it and only got rid of the guy as he struggled into the hotel by swinging one of these standing ashtrays at him. If it had been one of the players he would never have kicked a ball again. But that was Ned – hard as nails. The year before that in Barcelona he had a run in with Sammy in the dressing-room . They had a long-running feud from when Sam played for Rangers. Ned said, 'You outside, now!' Sammy wouldn't go with him and I can't blame him.

But that was Ned for you. Willie Ormond used to tell how Ned would look after him and Bobby Johnstone if anyone crocked them and also the time he blasted in a 30-yard free kick and he had a broken ankle at the time.

Another rough diamond was Bertie Auld. He was some player and as friendly as anything off the park. But when we played Middlesbrough in a pre-season friendly we just knew there would be trouble. Nobby Stiles did Bertie and broke his collar bone. I went over and told Bertie he had to go off. He refused: 'The wee bastard will be carried off before I walk off.' A few minutes later there was a 50-50 ball and Bertie let Stiles dive in and was waiting for him. As the dust settled Stiles was carried off screaming. You just didn't mess with Bertie. He was the dirtiest, sneakiest player around. Mind you if you were in a spot of bother Bertie would be first in for you.

Hibs was full of characters in those years. As I said more of a holiday camp than maybe it should have been, but it pro-duced some great football which was what the fans wanted to see. It is a tough game and a bit of a rat race.The sad thing is that it is only afterwards you really appreciate it. And it is only when you're gone the fans appreciate you.

CHAPTER SIX

CORKY

What was the greatest experience of Peter Cormack's career? Scoring against Real Madrid for Hibs, playing for Scotland against Pele and Brazil as a 19-year-old or winning the UEFA Cup with Liverpool? None of these actually (and this one's worth a few bob in the pub). The game in question was none other than the African Nations Cup tie between Botswana and Malawi. Peter Cormack was Botswana's manager that day as they won 2–0. Not a lot of people know that.

Peter was invited over, through the British Consul, for a five-week spell to coach them for this crunch game. 'It was an incredible experience. We won 2–0 in front of 36,000 people and I was presented to the Duke of Kent who was one of the visiting dignitaries.'

However it was just a one-off for Peter, a man often underestimated as both a coach and a player. Not long after the African experience he came back to Easter Road for a third spell, this time as coach with Alex Miller. There were three good years building Hibs up again until another one of these sudden splits that leaves a sour taste. However Peter prefers to maintain a dignified silence over the detail of what happened. 'It's something I am careful about discussing. I was really sorry when the split occurred because we were a good combination. That's as much as I am prepared to say on the record. It was handled very badly and the thing that hurt most was the way it affected my family. It took me a long time to get over the way they suffered.' It was a sad end for the man who had started his playing career in the early '60s and was brought back in 1979 by Eddie Turnbull to be groomed as a successor at the club.

It was during Walter Galbraith's tenure Peter arrived. A born and bred Leither his father was a staunch Hearts supporter but Peter was more interested in playing and would go instead to Easter Road for midweek games, particularly the European epics such as the battle with Barcelona.

Whatever people say about Walter Galbraith, he brought some tremendous players to Easter Road. Guys like Jim and Alex Scott, Gerry Baker, Willie Hamilton, Pat Quinn, Jim Easton, John Fraser, Neil Martin, Pat Stanton and Jimmy O'Rourke. And there were players already there like Eric Stevenson, a great winger and one who deserved to be capped for Scotland.

I was only 16 when I made my debut against Airdrie in a game Hibs lost 2–1 and was notable for Jim Easton breaking his leg.'

However big changes were ahead as Jock Stein took over at the beginning of the 1964/65 season. It was great for me at the start of my career to be managed by someone like Jock Stein and he created a real buzz at Easter Road. He thought big and brought Real Madrid to Easter Road for a friendly not long after he joined. For someone like me here was the chance to play against my idols. Di Stefano was injured but stars like Puskas, Gento and Santamaria were playing. We were the first British side they played on a European tour and had just come from France and Italy. That week Jock Stein worked hard with us on tactics. We knew they would want to play football, but we would make them play square and slow them down. People to this day still speak to me about that match. It really captured the public imagination. For the game we wore green shorts. After 15 minutes a long ball came through which Neil Martin knocked down to me and I scored with a left-footed volley. It was something you don't forget and we won 2–0. After the game we did a lap of honour round Easter Road. But it wasn't a one-off as we then went to Ibrox on the Saturday and beat Rangers 4–2. In a ten-day period we also played Celtic and beat them as well. It was just a sign of what a good manager Stein was and what a good team he was building. We could have gone and won the league and the Cup I'm sure, but Jock Stein's sudden departure was a disaster. It happened just before the semi-final against Dunfermline and you can't blame the players for losing 2–0 to them. We never played like we could and the team never really recovered. Stein leaving cost us the Cup. The timing of it all was incredible and it took a lot out of us. The whole business affected us a lot more than we realised at the time. We all had such a high respect for Jock Stein and I was fortunate to have played under such a manager even if it was only for such a short time. I also had the luck to play for the Shankly brothers, Bob at Hibs and Bill at Liverpool. They were different characters but they knew the game inside out. Both of them were also great friends with Jock Stein and were on the phone all the time.

In those early days I was just pleased to have broken through and I won an Under-23 cap. I had started as an outside right, but was moved in to centre forward where I would play with Neil Martin and Colin Stein as a joint striker. It was only at Liverpool that I was moved back to midfield.

These early days were good for me at Hibs and we played a lot of good attacking football with Bob Shankly. I was still a teenager when I won my first full cap and it could not have been against better opposition. Scotland played Brazil at Hampden in a warm-up for the World Cup in 1966. I was 19 and today that jersey still hangs in a cabinet in my house. There I was, still a laddie, playing against Pele and Gerson. But I feel I was very unfortunate in my international career as every time I got picked the manager was changed. John Prentice packed in just after the Brazil game and I was only to win nine caps under five different managers. Maybe if things had been more stable in that department I could have gone on and got 50 caps. At that time there were players like Bremner, Baxter and Charlie Cooke and I was the youngest of that group so often I was first to go with a new manager.

As a striker at Hibs I took a fair bit of stick, a lot more than a forward gets today so I had to look after myself. If I got a reputation for being a bit fiery it was because of that and I was a winner. There were times I retaliated and don't really regret it. You had to in a way to survive. There were guys like Roy Barry and John Greig and a couple of others around and you knew you were going to get it from them one way or the other at some time in a game. The first three or four times you went for the ball you would be up in the air.

But the eight years I spent in my first spell at Hibs were great years. I always relished playing Hearts and only lost once against them. That was my first derby when we lost 3–2 at Easter Road on New Year's Day although I scored, which I was to do regularly against them. There were also some great European ties. No one who was there could forget the Napoli game. Over in Italy we got a hiding and could not get the ball off them. We lost 4–1 and over here they thought the tie was finished. We could tell that when we saw their approach in a training session at Easter Road and their coach was up in the stand drinking a whisky. But we got off to the best of starts with

Bobby Duncan's long-range goal, then Pat Quinn scored just before half-time. In the dressing-room I remember saying that we just needed to get another one and we'd be level – and I got it. Alex Scott hit a cross to the far post and I headed it in. Although I was not tall I was good in the air and was known for scoring with my head. I did work on trying to hang there. I would study other players like Willie Bauld, Alan Gilzean and Neil Martin. A lot of it has to do with timing, making sure you are first up and using your arms. That way you are coming down as the other guys are jumping. Nobody coached me at it. It was just something I did myself. That night Pat Stanton got the fourth: another header. He was also very good in the air for someone who wasn't that tall. Colin Stein got the final goal to make it five.

We could not wait for the next round when we met Leeds. After a no-scoring draw at Elland Road, Leeds got a very dubious goal at Easter Road after Willie Wilson was pulled up for the four-step rule and Jack Charlton scored from the free kick. We should have gone further in Europe that year, but overall it was a great experience.

In the league there were high standards as well which a lot of people forget. Just about every team had quality players. Celtic had a great passer in Bobby Murdoch and Jimmy Johnstone was something else. Under Jock Stein they were becoming a great team. Rangers had Baxter and Willie Henderson, Aberdeen had Charlie Cooke and Davie Smith, Alex Edwards was at Dunfermline and Tommy McLean at Kilmarnock. At Hibs I was fortunate to play alongside forwards like Neil Martin, Joe McBride and Colin Stein. They would win it in the air and I would run on for it. I would say my best spell was with Colin.

Over the years there was always a lot of transfer talk surrounding me and after eight years I was sold to Nottingham Forest for £120,000. I had seen Colin Stein and Peter Marinello go and I was getting married and needed more money. There was speculation that Tottenham and Leeds were interested in me and I began to think: was it wise to stay at one club? I had been quite successful at Hibs but also wanted to develop as a player. At that time I don't think Hibs were ambitious enough and were too ready to sell players. People who go on about loyalty are talking rubbish. I loved Hibs, but I also wanted to find out how I would be with top players in England. I wanted to develop and I think I became a better player because of it.

England at that time was the top league in the world and I got the chance to play for Liverpool, one of the top clubs, not just in Britain but the world. All the stories about Bill Shankly were genuine. When I went to sign on with my father-in-law Shankly asked me what I had been doing to keep fit. I said that I had done some cross-country running. He said, 'This is Anfield, that is for the birds. The world snooker champion doesn't go swimming every day so do your work with a ball.' When Tony Hateley signed around that time he commented on the lovely lush grass. Shanks replied 'Aye son, don't worry about the grass. You've not come here to graze.'

I won two UEFA medals and an FA Cup medal with Liverpool. On the way to one of the UEFA medals we beat Hibs. Arthur Duncan scored at Easter Road and Mickey got one in reply to a hat-trick from Tosh at Anfield. Bill Shankly was quite a contrast to his brother Bob, but Bob had been very honest to me at Easter Road and knew his football. He spoke to Bill about me and that's one of the reasons Liverpool got interested.

When I was finishing my playing career with Bristol City I got the call to come back to Hibs. It had always been my ambition to be Hibs' manager so I came back and played for a short while. I got on well with Eddie Turnbull but he was not the man he had been. Without a doubt Eddie was a great coach. He was very highly thought of within the game and had been ahead of his time. But when I came back he was a changed man. Players who could pass were whacking the ball up the park, which would never have happened years earlier. Eddie had a bust-up with Tom Hart and my contract was then floating in mid-air. I was being groomed to be his successor as a coach but when they appointed Bertie Auld and gave him a five year contract I was in no-man's-land. My contract was then terminated and I went to manage Partick Thistle for three years and spent another two in Cyprus.

During that short spell back at Easter Road I played with George Best. He still had tremendous talent at that late stage in his career and was a smashing guy off the park. It was great to see his flashes of genius. When he was with Manchester United he had the most talent I had seen in any one player I had played against. Best ranks up there with Pele.

I loved my life as a footballer. Most players are great guys and will make anyone welcome at a new club. It's a big part of my life that can never be changed and although my main success was with Liverpool I look back on my time at Easter Road with fond memories. We had great laughs together and there was always something going on with Jimmy O'Rourke, Gerry Baker and Eric Stevenson around. The usual practical jokes were part of it all – somebody's shirt sleeves getting cut, shoes in the bath etc. We were always winding Willie Hamilton up and one time persuaded him to go upstairs to see Jock Stein about a bonus. Willie knocked on the door and Jock calls him in without raising his head. 'Something you want?' 'Aye, boss, I wanted to see about a bonus.' Jock kept writing and said 'If you are not down the stairs by the time I lift my head I'll throw you down.'

These were great days and football was not as serious as it is today. Gerry Baker was another joker and he was the fastest player I have ever seen, a lot quicker even than his brother Joe. One day Gerry and Willie decided to wind up Johnny Byrne who was quick over ten yards. Gerry would lie down with his head on the byeline and give him ten yards of start and still beat him.

He fell for it so Willie got Tam McNiven to bring the wages out for everyone and to be starter. Willie was running a book as Tam fired the gun. You would have had to see it to believe it, all the players roaring them on as Gerry beat him.

They were a really great bunch of guys, Jimmy O'Rourke, Pat Stanton, Eric Stevenson, Pat Quinn – a player who could see a pass when no one else could. But Willie Hamilton was something else. So many times you would come out to training and he would be hanging over the wall being sick. Then he'd turn round wiping his mouth: 'That's me, I'm fine now' and start training with the rest of us.

It was a fabulous life and I made a lot of friends.

When the chance came to return to Easter Road for a third time I felt I was ready. John Greig had put Alex Miller onto me. I had been coaching for five years which is what it takes to learn the trade and how to handle players one-on-one, delegate responsibility, organise the club and know who to trust and when to trust people. All the time you are still learning and never really relaxed in the early years. However there were things I had learned from when I was a player. If I lost in those days I would not go out. But as a manager I learned to look to next week and the next game immediately.

The split with Alex Miller is something between ourselves. Whatever our differences he is the first manager to win something at Easter Road since the early '70s. He has done well with what he has got and he has not done any worse than you would expect. I know many of these players' strengths and weaknesses. When I was working with him there were young players already there, but there was no youth policy and something had to be done about that. But it is not an easy process. There are not as many good young players about as there were 20 years ago and there is more pressure nowadays with the Premier Division. It's difficult to bring 16- or 18-year-olds through. One youngster who has done it at Hibs since my time is Gordon Hunter. He's a good defender who has been steady over the seasons for Hibs, while a player like Mickey Weir has faded in recent times. Mickey has a lot of talent but he has never fulfilled it properly. It would be a let-down both for him and Hibs supporters to see it wasted, but it is up to Mickey himself now to do something about it.

With limited resources Alex Miller and I got Hibs going again. Early on I went down to England to see a striker when I spotted this other player, Gareth Evans. Somebody told me the wee blond boy had some pace which George McCluskey at that time lacked up front. So I came back and told Alex about him and how he would be going for a song. Alex went down with Jim Gray and signed him for £25,000.

We were always on the lookout for a bargain. A friend gave me a call about Pat McGinlay and we went and had a look at him. He was a good athlete and had plenty of potential. Hibs got him for nothing off Blackpool – another bit of good business.

But of all the real talent at Easter Road in recent times Andy Goram stands out. I phoned Joe Royle who I knew from my Bristol days. Joe was reluctant to let him go but said he'd let me know as his chairman was pressing him to sell. He called me and said that if we were prepared to pay £300,000 Goram was ours. I said 'Let's go for him', and when Alex met him Goram signed after chatting for half an hour. 'Come up here', we said, 'and you'll be in the shop window for a Scotland place'. Andy was a big favourite. He's a likeable rogue and a good pro. Hibs sold him for £1 million and he became Scotland's number one. Another good bit of business.

On top of that we got Hibs back into Europe for the first time in over a decade and a lot of that was thanks to Steve Archibald.

To be fair we got him due to David Duff and Jim Gray. We knew it would take Stevie about six weeks to get fit, but it was worth the wait. He was a superb player and offered an awful lot. He was undoubtedly the best player I have worked with as a coach. His 16 goals that season were vital to Hibs.

Despite some letdowns football's been good to me, but my biggest disappointment is I never won anything for the Hibs supporters. As a player I always thought of that. I wanted to be a hero to the fans, winning a league championship or the Cup. We did win the Summer Cup in 1964 and I scored in that final against Aberdeen but it wasn't a big trophy. In my eight years the team should have done better, but it was always breaking up with somebody moving on. However, Hibs have been such a big part of my life and that will never change.

CARRICKNOWE BUILDING SERVICES LIMITED

40 Oxgangs Bank, Edinburgh EH13 9LH

Telephone: 0131-445 5322/5378.

Fax: 0131-445 5553

MAIN BUILDING

CONTRACTORS

ALL

CONTRACT WORK

UNDERTAKEN

CHAPTER SEVEN

THE QUIET MAN

Every era has its own heroes, but there are special players who bridge the generation gap. At the Hibs concert at the Usher Hall in May 1995 stars dating back from the '40s to the present day paraded on stage to acclaim from a full house. But the biggest cheer of the evening was reserved for Patrick Gordon Stanton. Pat himself was taken aback especially in the company of Smith, Reilly and Baker but the Niddrie boy still holds a special place among today's Hibs supporters.

Throughout the '60s and '70s he was Hibs, and for a brief shining moment Hibs hearts rose again when he became manager in the early '80s. Then the dream turned sour. But no one can take away the memory of the grace, style, dignity and touch of steel the 'Quiet Man' brought to Easter Road.

Pat was signed by Walter Galbraith but his career really began to take off when Jock Stein arrived.

Looking back to that time, a game that really stands out was the one against Real Madrid. Jock Stein had just taken over at Easter Road and we won the Summer Cup. Hearts were in Europe that year and we weren't, but in a typical Stein move he decided to stage a big European night at Easter Road. Who better to get than Real Madrid? They were the most famous club in the world at the time and it really upstaged Hearts. The press was full of it for weeks in the build-up. Stein was always a master at handling the press.

It turned out to be a really magical night. They may have been just past their best but it was some feeling to be standing out there, yards away from them just before kick-off. That night I was to pick up Puskas. The day before Stein had us out on the park and gave us a loose framework of how they were going to play. Naturally enough I had been looking forward to it and it was not just because we were wearing green shorts for the first time. I remember we were first out and it was quite a while before they appeared. Normally when you are kicking about before a game you just continue warming up when the other side comes out and don't really pay any attention to them. But that night even we stopped to watch along with the crowd as they came out of the tunnel. They looked like gods, all in white. But they were soon brought down to earth down the slope at Easter Road and the game worked out exactly as Stein said it would. He had told me where Puskas would play and warned us about them coming at us in threes and fours. He told us to dig in, not dive in. If we could hold out and not let them over-run us then the game would start to turn our way.

The thing you have to remember about that Hibs team was that there were some very good players in it and outstanding ones like Willie Hamilton. I think Willie turned it on a bit more that night because he was up against Puskas. He was that sort of a guy. Willie could have played against anyone and he would have thought he was as good if not better. He was some man, was Willie. One of the things that really sticks out was when they got a late corner. Willie came back into the box, a rare event in itself. 'What was he doing there?' I thought he might be having a rest somewhere else. The fans probably thought Willie was one of the senior pros coming back to encourage us young lads to hold on and keep calm. But he strolled up and said: 'Hey, Pat son, they tell me you get a watch for playing this lot.'

The thing was he was right. I still have mine and it keeps good time, but that was Willie for you. The only things that got Willie overexcited weren't on a football park.

Other very good players in that side were Pat Quinn, John Parke the full back, Neil Martin, Peter Cormack and Eric Stevenson.

I got a wee insight early on into Puskas when he went over the top on me. I was a bit taken aback. Here was the world-famous player sorting out me, a young laddie from Niddrie. But I realised he hadn't survived all these years at the top without being able to give it out and look after himself. I was only 18 at the time but I knew enough to hold back and watch out for their one-twos. The only way a one-two works is if you are sucked in towards the ball. They didn't like getting beaten that night and showed in some ways that they were just like any other players with a wee bit of bad temper here and there. Anyway we won 2–0 and did a wee lap of honour afterwards.

The thing about Jock Stein was that he had come and made a successful team out of virtually the same players who had been struggling with relegation the season before. Here we were beating Real Madrid yet a few months before we had been struggling against Queen of the South and Raith Rovers. In one season he turned us around and if he had stayed we could well have won a league and Cup double. But everyone knows about the bad timing of his move to Celtic as far as Hibs was concerned. Stein also went on to do the same with Celtic. The Lisbon Lions were for the most part guys who had been at Parkhead before he arrived. Although he was a special manager so much of what he did was common sense.

The Saturday after we beat Real Madrid we played Rangers. I had never been at Ibrox in my life yet we went and won 4–2. We were up against marvellous players like Jim Baxter, Ian McMillan and Jimmy Millar. However, the interesting thing to a young player like me was that some of the name players were not that good close up, but those three I mentioned were special. Again Willie Hamilton was revved up before that game and was winding up Jim Baxter in the tunnel. And sure enough Willie came out on top. I suppose Willie thought if he could take care of Puskas, Baxter would be no problem either and he was right.

The Real game made a lot of people sit up and that and the Rangers game made us think what could be done. We beat Rangers three times that season and feared no one. But when Stein went it was a huge disappointment. It was a really strange time to leave and we went on to lose to Dunfermline in the Cup semi-final at Tynecastle. Celtic beat them in the final with McNeill's last minute-goal and that was the start of their great run. Back at Easter Road we could not understand why it could not be left till the end of the season. But maybe Willie Harrower thought, like Rangers did with Souness, that once Stein wanted to go then the break should be made as quickly as possible.

Bob Shankly who took over was a similar type of man to Stein – straightforward with a great love of the game. They were good friends and I think Stein recommended him. But he was a lot quieter than Stein who was so charismatic. However we had some good runs with Bob and he was a great believer in attacking football. He never had time for the 'hammer throwers' as he called them. The Napoli game is one of the classics from that period that people still speak to me about. Although we lost

4–1 over there it could have been 4–4 and we were confident we would win at home. They made a big mistake as they left their match winner Altafini behind. When he scored in Naples he was away round behind the goals celebrating when we kicked off and went up the park to score. It's a pity Juventus never made that mistake a few seasons later when Altafini came back to haunt us, scoring two at Easter Road. I must say he was one of the best I played against. But the night before the Napoli second leg their manager was so relaxed he was up in the directors' box with a large whisky watching them. I'll tell you one thing: he needed another large one after we were finished with them the next night.

The crucial thing that night was the first goal from Bobby Duncan. He hit it from nowhere. It was so spectacular that it lifted the whole place. You just had that feeling: aye-aye, here we go. If it had been a trundler or a more ordinary goal it would not have set the whole thing off. It gave everyone a lift. But there were no great celebrations afterwards. Not like players today. It was straight home to Craigmillar for me. I got a lift from George McNeill. He dropped me off at Niddrie Crossroads without stopping. Knowing George I don't think he even slowed down. I never even got a chance to have a fish supper to celebrate. Now if George had dropped me at the Bingham tunnel I could have as there's a chippie there.

Things, as you can see, were a lot more humble in those days. Today's players are all going to places like Bermuda on holiday. In those days only the players with money went to Majorca while a lot of our lads were off to Butlins. A lot of us didn't have cars. It shows how things have changed. There's a picture in the book *The Quiet Man* where John McNamee had got a car – just an ordinary Ford but it created quite a stir as you can tell by the crowd gathered round.

When the Scotland players' hotel was robbed in Finland not long ago it showed how times had changed. Money was stolen and credit cards taken along with their jewellery . . . their jewellery? In our days if someone had broken into our rooms they would have left money for you. No one was going to steal Timex watches or postal orders from yer ma. Now it's Rolexes, gold chains, American Express, but good luck to them. Players are treated like celebrities now. In our days it just didn't happen. The first hotel I was ever in with Hibs the waitress asked me if I wanted a black or white coffee. I didn't know what she was on about. We drank tea in the house. Being an experienced traveller I said 'White' and it was only when I got it I realised it was one with milk. That was at the Scotia Hotel in Great King Street with Eric Stevenson and Willie Wilson. We used to go back there and get a meal after the game. But the club was rich in character in those days with a few rascals too. There were boys like big John McNamee. He had a magnificent physique and was great in the air, but he was also a great passer of the ball. If big John had to play Rangers every Saturday he would have been a world beater. I remember him scoring against Rangers with a header and whacking John Greig one with his elbow at the same time and telling him 'Aye, that'll sink yer submarine.'

Willie Hamilton was one of the best I ever played with. Stein thought he was something else. When I was at Celtic, Tommy Burns and Roy Aitken once asked me who was the best I'd played with and I said maybe I wouldn't like to single out one player but Willie Hamilton might be it. They didn't really know who Willie was, but just then big Stein came dripping out of the shower. He had overheard the question and had come to back me up.

Another player who deserves more recognition than he got was Eric Stevenson. Eric was a great player. I often say a lot of wingers are not too clever, but you couldn't say that about Stevie, he read the game very well. A lot of people forget that Eric got a bad leg-break early on in his career which set him back a bit.

A real help to the younger boys when I started out was Tommy Preston. It's sad that a guy like Tommy with a lot to offer the club was never used as he should have been.

One of the best bits of advice I ever got was around that time from Willie Toner who had come to Hibs from Kilmarnock. Willie said that when you got on to the park you shouldn't have your mind made up on what you were going to do: it doesn't happen that way. What he was meaning was you had to adapt as you went along. I had played well the week before and he was trying to point out it would not be the same this week. John Grant, was right back and Ronnie Simpson in goal.

In one of my first games Gordon Smith was playing for Dundee and you could see he was still a great player. I remember at one stage he pulled my jersey. If he really wanted it all he needed to do was ask. But Gordon was a truly marvellous player and could have done Hibs a lot of good for a few more years. But he did himself a lot of good, winning another couple of league medals at Hearts and Dundee.

And of course there was Mr O'Rourke. He and I hung around together and to this day I still cannae get rid of him. It's only when you think back that you appreciate the good times we had together. A seven-week tour of America with the likes of Jimmy O'Rourke is an adventure in itself. But O'Rourke is another who was a better player than a lot of people gave him credit for. He was a great schoolboy player and started like a bomb with Hibs. He was only 16 and he played in Europe against Utrecht. He'd played for Holy Cross school one week and the next he was playing for Hibs. Like Eric he got a really bad injury early on in his career at Tannadice which affected his career for a long time. Because of Jimmy's power and strength the less cultured eye would miss out on his skill and touch. But he was some boy at the free kicks and could curl them in like a Continental, a feat you still don't really see in Scottish football.

The first time we went to America was some event. We used to pick Jock Stein up at his house on the Queensferry Road en route to a game and this day he got in and just said 'How would you like to go to America?' Well it gave the Butlin's brigade some lift over the next few games. That was typical Stein. He knew how to throw something in as a wee bit of motivation. However he never made the trip with us as he'd left for Celtic before the summer.

The first team we played on tour was Nottingham Forest in Vancouver and Joe Baker was playing for Forest. We played all over Canada and went down to New York. At that time not many people went to America and, although we got up to a lot of nonsense, we saw a lot as well. Not many people in Edinburgh had been to an Indian reservation or to Harlem. It was all new and just like the films for us laddies from Craigmillar and Clermiston.

Jimmy was really taken with the bell hops racing round paging everyone just as in the films. He set up one of the directors on the trip, Bob Pownie, as his wind-up. In every hotel where we went a bell hop would come through paging Bob Pownie just as he was about to sit down to dinner. Before long Bob was groaning each time 'It's that wee bastard O'Rourke again'.

Everwhere we went it was amazing how people would come up to you with some connection with Hibs. We also went to Nigeria during the civil war with Biafra. The first day there I got a knock on the door and there's this boy from Craigmillar, a friend of my brothers, who had heard we were in town. It was quite scarey that trip with the civil war going on and there were a lot of road blocks. That was where we got accused of being British mercenaries. After the first game we'd done not too well and Bob Shankly came in and said 'No wonder they think you're mercenaries and not footballers, they must have seen you play.'

In Ghana a decision went against us and one of the team called the ref a black bastard. He just turned round and said 'You white bastard' and played on. What would you have to do to get sent off in Ghana?

These travels were all part of the tradition at Hibs built up by the Famous Five in the '50s for travelling abroad. But the biggest game for many Hibs fans is no more than couple of miles across town. The Edinburgh derby was good to me as a player and Tynecastle was a ground I hardly ever lost at. There was never any nastiness about derbies in those days. As a laddie I went to games together with Hearts pals from Craigmillar with no need for segregation.

They were tough affairs to play in and the one everyone wants to talk about is the 7–0 game. My memory of that is how my mate O'Rourke stole my chance of a goal by sliding in to help the ball over the line. He's always been a greedy so-and-so. Jimmy did not have a bad record against Hearts and had scored two along with Stevie to put Hibs four up in the first ten minutes a few years before at Tynecastle. But we took our foot off the pedal that day.

After the 7–0 game we were so complacent that Hearts won the next derby 4–1. The next time we made sure we would not slip up and won 3–1 at the New Year. The thing about the 7–0 game was we could all feel something like that was coming. We had just won the League Cup, beaten Ayr 8–1 and run up big scores against Sporting Lisbon and FC Besa. The Ayr game was the first one after the League Cup final and Eddie Turnbull was determined we would put on a good performance. Ally McLeod, who was Ayr manager at the time, said afterwards we were   better than Real Madrid. Well, we knew that already as we'd beaten them a few years before.

We also had a really good game with Aberdeen just before the derby, winning 3–2 and on New Year's Day Jimmy said we were really going to catch somebody and it just happened to be Hearts.

Hearts could actually have been a goal or two up before we scored, but then again we could have got ten that day. At half time Turnbull told us to keep going and not let up. But I suppose we did a bit although we kept creating chances. And that was when O'Rourke proved he was some mate by sliding in to nick my goal! But we would have learned more from that game if they had beaten us. You never pick up much from giving somebody a hammering. Unlike today there weren't any players lounges then so we didn't mix with the Hearts players afterwards which is just as well on an occasion like that. Coming from Craigmillar most of my mates were Hearts supporters so it's something you didn't want to rub in. The score spoke for itself. You didn't need to say anything. But I remember my father saying after that 4–0 game at Tynecastle when we toyed with Hearts and took the mickey that it was a terrible thing to do. You should never humiliate fellow professionals,. It is something I kept in mind and I wouldn't like to think in the 7–0 game we did that. All we were concentrating on was winning as well as possible.

One of my goals at Tynecastle which is mentioned to me most is the one I scored a couple of years later in the 94th minute. It earned us a draw. Those were the days of five o'clock opening and Hearts fans used to say to me 'Remember you scored when the pubs were open.'

It was during that period when Hibs played some of their best European football and we beat Sporting Lisbon and Besa by six and seven goals respectively. But the best European performance was the away match in Lisbon even though we lost. We wore purple jerseys that night and could have played anyone. There were 100,000 spectators and they were a very good team. Under that pressure away from home we held on well despite losing two goals and Arthur pulled one back late on. However we'd gone at them right from the start and Alex Cropley hit the post in the first ten minutes. But everything went right that night including our individual performances and overall organisation. They made the mistake of thinking the one goal lead might be enough and were happy to be drawing at Easter Road. But they let it drop which is the worst thing you can do. We did it in the derby after the 7–0 game when we lost 4–1 to Hearts. You keep trying to shake yourself but it is almost as if you can do nothing about it. The main thing a team must do is make sure they are in the right frame of mind.

With guys in your team like Hateley at Rangers, Robson at Manchester United, Dave Mackay at Hearts, Baresi at Milan nobody will have to tell them how to play. The manager knows they will just go out and do it. The trick is to have enough in your team like them so that you don't have to worry. They reckon if at least seven are on form you should be all right. It's too much to expect every player to be on peak form, but if the manager is forever having to cajole players, it's no use. Of course, there are players who need it but the key to a successful team is to have enough who don't. Even your successful managers like Alex Ferguson, Stein and the like can't go and give a rousing speech every Saturday. A big part of the managing is getting the right blend.

In the current Hibs team a player like Hunter will perform for you every week. But the secret in football, as with any other form of management, is to get good people working with you on and off the park. Guys you could rely on like that in my early days were John Grant (an underrated player), Bobby Duncan, O'Rourke and John Blackley. The recent Manchester United team are an example. They have several like Bruce, Irwin, and Keane that they could count on. Ramsay made that choice in 1966 when he left out Greaves – a marvellous player but you were not sure what you were going to get from him – but he knew that Roger Hunt and Geoff Hurst would give him what he wanted.

There's the Bill Shankly story about how he had a scout watch someone a few times and asked if he liked him. The scout said: 'Well, eh.' Shankly butted in: 'That'll do me. Forget it.' You need to know straight off.It's a strange thing what makes a player. Some can be great in training but can never produce the same on the day. But you can tell who the real pro is. He starts preparing himself mentally about Wednesday for a game and he's ready for it come Saturday.

You can spot these real pros in training. They never skive. The skiver will only do 18 press-ups but they'll do 22. They'll run round the cone at the corner but the skiver will cut it. If he does that week in week out he'll also do it on a Saturday. I think supporters can tell. Mind you I feel I was accepted easily at Easter Road because I was a local lad. I got away with things that others might not have done such as the penalty miss against Leeds. If it had been another player say on his way to get the train back to Glasgow he might have been strung up in Leith Walk on the nearest lamp post. But very few people mentioned it to me. When we went to extra-time in that game against Leeds, Eddie nominated the five and said: 'You take the first one.' I turned round but there was nobody behind me. He was pointing at me. I sent the goalie the wrong way but hit the post. The last one Bremner hit the bar, but it caught the underside and went in. What annoyed me more than anything was that game should never have gone to extra-time.

That Hibs team, although it had great players, maybe did not have enough of these types I have been speaking about. It's no secret there was no love lost between Eddie Turnbull and me but one thing about him you could never dispute was that he had forgotten more about football than most people ever know. Tactically he was very astute but he fell down in man management. Eddie would never have won any prizes at charm school and was of the old school believing you ruled by fear and discipline. But I've always believed there is more to management than that. You can't treat everyone the same. The way Alex Ferguson treats Cantona is a perfect example as was the way big Stein dealt with Jimmy Johnstone and Willie Hamilton. But that Hibs team's failure to win the league or Cup was not Eddie Turnbull's fault. It was the players who let him down. He made a mistake in breaking us up too early but I think he thought we were never going to do it.

CHAPTER EIGHT

EVERYONE KNOWS HIS NAME

If ever there was a player Hibs fans thought of as one of us it was Jimmy O'Rourke. At times in the good old days of the Cave you almost got the impression it was half full of O'Rourkes, Jimmy's brothers. And all of us knew that if Jimmy cut, he'd bleed green! That's why the fans loved him.

The Clermiston dynamo was a boy wonder at Holy Cross school where he caught Hibs' eye along with clubs such as Manchester United and Celtic. Jimmy recalls those days:

I remember the first time I was picked for the team two years ahead of me and the team-sheet went up. The captain was Pat Stanton and there were also Jimmy McManus, Davy Hogg and Malcolm McPherson, who is now dead, who went on to play at some stage for Hibs. It was Hugh Shaw who signed me provisionally as a schoolboy for Hibs and it was Douglas Fairbanks, sorry Walter Galbraith, who was manager when I made my debut.

Other clubs were interested in me, namely Celtic and Manchester United. I went down to see United and also went through with my father to Parkhead. Bob Kelly the chairman said to me 'You're a Catholic so you'll want to sign for Celtic.' Well that was something we just weren't into and we walked out of the door. Anyway we were Hibs people first and foremost.

At home in the bedroom there was a picture of the Sacred Heart on the wall and my brothers and I took it down and put up a picture of Joe Baker. We got a right cuffing for that, but Joe was still our hero, if not our God.

Pat and Davy Hogg, with whom I'd played at school broke into the Hibs team at around the same time as me. But I couldn't believe it when I got picked to play against Utrecht in the Fairs Cup in 1962. I was only 16, and the youngest Hibs player to play in Europe. The game bypassed me in some ways but I do remember hitting the bar with a header as we won 2–1. But the next round we got gubbed 5–0 away by Valencia. It was possibly all a bit much for me. A group of young players had all broken through because there had been a lot of injuries. I was the youngest and had scored in my first-team debut against Dunfermline. But that season was touch and go as we skirted with relegation, but we beat Raith 4–0 in that famous crunch game to stay up. One guy who helped me a lot in those early days was Eric Stevenson, especially when I broke my leg in my second season against Dundee United in the League Cup.

Hibs went on to the semis in the year 1963/64 season only to lose to Morton in the semi-final. But Stevie was a special player and I reckon he's the best uncapped winger Scotland ever had.

That leg break was a big setback and it took about four years for me to really recover my form and get my career going again. But although these were a tough few years they had their highlights, such as the derby game we won 4–0 in 1965. Eric and I both scored twice in the first ten minutes. At the time I was playing in the reserves. John Fraser told me I was not playing that Saturday and I assumed I'd been dropped from the reserves, so I planned to go down to Blackpool for the September weekend. But Neil Martin was injured and I was to report with the first team to Tynecastle. I well remember Roy Barry trying to do me in that game, but it made little difference. I scored one with my left from 25 yards and then just to even things up the next with my right from 25 yards. I reckoned Hearts were sponsored for inhalers that day as we gave them the runaround and they were chasing us for the final 80 minutes. We'd cuffed them good and proper with ten minutes gone. But I also didn't miss out on my Blackpool weekend driving down after the game. Mind you I was dropped for the next game. Over that spell I was often reserve and there was a hell of a bunch of good players around like Peter Cormack, Willie Hamilton, Neil Martin, Colin Stein, Pat Quinn and Eric in the forward line. We fairly rattled in the goals and had a lot of good times together especially on these long close season tours of America.

Willie Hamilton was in his element on these occasions. There's the story of the time he bent the silver salver he'd won as man of the match to squeeze it into his bag. Willie was something else. Another time we were invited over to take part in a Scottish week in Cannes. Pipers welcomed us and as we got to the hotel dray men were delivering kegs of Scottish beer. Two minutes later Willie was missing. The search party didn't take long to find him down in the cellars with the dray men having a bevvy. He'd just followed the roll of the barrel.

Willie wasn't the only character about at that time. Big John McNamee was another one: a right rough diamond and a wee bit huffy. In training he used to say 'Youse against us, Catholic versus Protestants'. You'd never seen so many conversions. I was always sure to remind John I'd been an altar boy.

Football was a lot harder then than it is today. John Madsen arrived from Denmark and one of his first games was away to Airdrie. He was up against Derek Whiteford, another rough diamond. At half time Madsen was sitting in the dressing-room muttering 'I quit, I quit'.

During these years I didn't get the long run in the side I wanted and when Bob Shankly was manager he played me wide on the right. I hated it. It wasn't my position. As a result, I missed out on one of the Easter Road epics against Napoli. I got a game in the first leg. They went 4–0 up and Altafini was off the park kissing the crowd when we kicked off and went up to score through Colin Stein. I was dropped for the replay but that night, when Bobby Duncan opened the scoring, must be one of the best ever at Easter Road.

One good point I picked up in those years was from Joe McBride. He took me aside and told me I was trying too hard. 'You're trying to make every goal a World Cup goal. I'll show you how to pass it into the net. First and foremost make sure it's on target then it's 50-50 whether it will be a goal. It's all up to the goalie then. There's no need to try a screamer every time. Place it, use the side foot.' It was good advice, a seasoned pro giving a wayward laddie the benefit of his experience. It helped me a lot.

Big changes came when Eddie Turnbull took over. He brought discipline, organisation and great tactical knowledge. He worked us unbelievably hard. He was so meticulous and worked for hours on a system of wave after wave of attacks. He made you aware of so much about football that you'd never realised before.

I remember not long after he arrived we went to Ayr. They had not a bad side in those days with Ally McLeod as manager and Johnny Doyle and Dixie Deans in their side. They went ahead, then I equalised when I hit the bar, then dived into the ruck to head in the rebound. It was quite a good result and I knew I had had a good game. When Pat, Alan Gordon and I were getting dropped off at the Barnton Hotel ET grabbed my arm. 'By Christ, Jimmy, you'll sleep well tonight. You worked like a Trojan.' I felt great. I was dropped the following week. That was ET for you. Nobody got on with him, but I feel he made me a far better player than I might have been. He was some man, but could he read the game? When we played Sporting Lisbon it was 1–1 at half-time. Alan had scored for us and Gesualde for them. I was having a nightmare and Eddie told us we were playing worse than if we were a man short. He switched Arthur Duncan to the right and the first time Arthur got down the wing and the ball came over I scored. Eddie did that a lot and he always seemed to know to do it at the right time.

We used to have a laugh at him as he was so serious. Mind you never to his face, do you think we were daft? In the away tie against Sporting Lisbon they gave us watches as presents and we gave them tartan rugs. Eddie began ranting and raving at half-time and waving his arms around and his new watch went flying across the room. There was silence as Johnny Hamilton said: 'Hey boss, doesn't time fly.' Needless to say ET didn't appreciate that. He never did see the funny side. Another time he had the blackboard up for a tactics talk and he was demonstrating a free kick and saying 'Find Bishy,' pointing at one of the magnetic discs. He went on to corners when the magnet fell off. Stan Vincent interrupted: 'He boss, Bishy's on the floor.'

I have great memories of these days and they are so clear because my family shared so much of it being a Hibs-daft family. We have a laugh when my brothers Michael, Billy and John remember incidents such as the semi-final against Rangers in the League Cup when a Rangers fan started calling me a fenian bastard. One of my brothers was going to have go at him for slagging me. Then another one jumps in 'You can slag my brother but never my ma.' I think the guy wished he'd kept his mouth shut. If you know my brothers you'll know what I mean. There was another family story of my cousin Willie's wedding which was on the day of the League Cup final. They had a radio on and when they were cutting the cake I scored. There was a roar at the reception and the cheering went on throughout the wedding.

Our League Cup victory was well deserved. We had lost the

cup final 6–1 to Celtic only a few months before. That game could have finished 8–4 and we squandered quite a few chances that day. But we maintained our belief in our own ability and got back at Celtic quickly, winning the Drybrough Cup and then came our League Cup run. By the time we won it we were really something with a great game at Airdrie in the quarter finals and then Rangers in the semis.

The week after the final we beat Ayr 8–1 then Aberdeen 3–2. Hearts supporters were afraid to go up the town at that time.

There was a tremendous spirit in the squad and real camaraderie. Although we did not win as much as we should have that team gave a lot of enjoyment to a lot of people and we had a great time doing it. Then came the climax of that period with the New Year derby. We trained hard on the morning of 1 January. ET growled at us with pride: 'There's no other team in Britain training this morning.' I remember looking at the television that day and Zorro was on. There was something about that Z that kept flashing up that was an omen. I see it now: it was really a seven.

I picked up the boys at the Barnton Hotel that day where a few of us met. It was my turn to drive. When everybody got in I said 'I've got a funny feeling. Somebody's been due a going over from us and are really going to catch it. Today's the day.' Well, everybody who speaks to me about that game says we could have scored more. I think a lot of Hibs fans would like to have seen us score ten, but seven's got a nice ring to it. But at the end of the day that afternoon at Tynecastle I was only doing my job. Mind you, I showed my feelings a bit when Alan headed in the seventh and I followed up to batter it into the roof of the net.

It was some team we had and like most of the players I felt it was broken up too early. There was a great spirit among us all. Pat and I have always been big mates and we used always to room together. Pat was very dry and really witty, great at the one-liner. Johnny Hamilton was a typical Glaswegian and a real comic as was big Jim Black in a different way. We went to Benidorm once and there was this doctor from London we got to know in the hotel. Lying at the poolside one day the doc says: 'Chaps, can I make a pertinent point. I have watched you very closely now for seven days. You hardly eat a thing, never go to bed and drink to excess. As a professional I was wondering how long this can last.' Big Jim says all indignant: 'At least another ten days, mon, until we gae hame.'

Jim had a lot of talent as well. But I suppose John Brownlie was the most skilful at the back, but he was better attacking than most forwards. And alongside was Sloop, one of the hardest tacklers you could come across. Unfortunately he didn't even let up in training. In midfield there were three special players. Alex Cropley was magnificent perhaps in some ways like John Collins today. Alex was as good as John, if not better. Everyone knows how good Mickey Edwards was and then we had Arthur on the wing. We never knew what he was going to do but neither did the opposition. And then there was my partnership with Alan Gordon up front. We worked very hard on waves of attacks with the back four coming forward. At first I would go a bit early for the ball, but more and more we worked on playing at right angles and timing my running onto lay-offs to perfection. Everyone remembers Alan's aerial power but he was underestimated on the ground. Despite what ET said he did have clever feet. That team should have been left together for one more year at least. There was no complacency amongst us and we had the right balance of skill and strength. But ET was the boss and made the decisions.

However, another vital part of the make-up of Hibs in that era was the board led by Tom Hart. He loved Hibs as much as I did. He wanted Hibs to be right up at the top of Scottish football and everything about the club had to be first class. We were in New York once and the hotel we were booked into wasn't that good, but it was passable. Tom Hart immediately grabbed the courier 'Do you ken who you are dealing with son? This is the famous Hibs FC. Get us booked into the best hotel in New York'. I don't think the boy kent who or what Hibs were, but he got the message and we were soon on our way to a five-star hotel. But that was typical of the chairman. His attitude was that Hibs would never play second fiddle to anyone and only the best was good enough. Big Stewartie used to say certain people couldn't even spell Hibs to Tom Hart.

Of course I never wanted to leave Hibs when I did, but a player hasn't a lot of say once the manager's set on something. Meanwhile, knocks I'd taken along the way were to bring an end to my career. I had three leg breaks in all and the injury that finished me came ironically from my supposed mate big George Stewart. By now I was playing for St Johnstone and it was against Hibs of all people at Easter Road that it happened. I suppose it was fitting I should bring the curtain down on my career there. Going in for a ball with the big man I tried to give him a wee dunt, but George lunged through and my knee popped out. The referee shouted for the trainer and my old pal Tam McNiven raced on before the St Johnstone trainer could get to me. Tam was the best physio of all time in my book. I went to Monklands Hospital as a result of the injury and the surgeon said 'I see you've injured this leg before but somebody worked on it'. I told him about Tam. 'Well, Mr O'Rourke,' he said 'you can thank him for adding on five or six years to your career.'

Tam was a good guy if maybe a bit soft with us. Once we were in Blackpool with Bob Shankly and went for walk in the park after lunch before the evening's games. Instead of a relaxing stroll Tam caved in to let us loose on the shows and we went wild on the roller coaster, the big wheel, the lot. That night we lost 5–0. I've got trouble with my knee to this day with arthritis but it would be a lot worse if it wasn't for Tam. But a lot of the blame lies with myself for practising shapes at the back of Easter Road on the concrete ever since I was a ground staff laddie.

A lot of that training amongst yourselves, such as head tennis perfects your skills and you have a great time and build up team spirit. At times today I feel that Largs has hijacked the game and that there is a system that you have to use. When George and I joined Pat at Easter Road when he was manager we would try a few new things that weren't in the coaching manuals. One of my pet hates of the Largs school was corners where everyone had to be back in his own box. I used to think: 'Why not stick three or four men on the half-way line?' In the season we were with Pat we did not get relegated, but we also had no chance of Europe. In this game we were playing Dundee United who won the Premier League that year. We went up to Tannadice and Ralph Callachan was due to play behind the front two. Stewartie said: 'What about playing five up?' Remember we were playing the league leaders away. Anyway we went and did it and we drew 3–3 and gave them a real hard game. Their players were totally confused as they didn't know how to handle it and Jim McLean conceded afterwards that we'd out-thought him.

I thought we did reasonably well in that short period and it was just a pity we weren't working together in better circumstances. But a legacy of Pat's astuteness was the players he brought through, such as Mickey Weir, Kano, Gordon Hunter and John Collins. Pat also made a great buy in Alan Rough. He could have played Brazil every week and it would have made no difference to Roughie. We also tried to stay true to the Hibs spirit and did have some high scoring games such as the 8–1 win over Kilmarnock.

When I was on the coaching staff at Easter Road my forte was with the younger players such as Mickey and Kano. We used to have five-a-sides of me, Ralph, Jackie, George and Pat versus Mickey, Kano, Kevin McKee, John Collins and Geebsie after the training had finished. We'd strive to beat them and didn't give them a thing. They probably found it quite funny taking on these old guys. But we would always try and guide them, give them confidence and through that gain respect. I spent a lot of time with them and felt I had a job to enlighten them . Each laddie has a different nature, home life etc and you have to appreciate that in the way you treat them. You build up camaraderie amongst them.

One of the most important things to point out is that anyone can play when you are winning but when you are a goal down away to Dumbarton or Airdrie and the sleet's lashing down, that's the time the real players get going.

I believe Hibs main tradition is as pioneers at the forefront of Scottish football. We have always been renowned for our attacking football and I think you're obliged to give the punters respect and value for money. The Hibs supporters have their views and they need to be heeded. They have always wanted attacking football. That's the true Hibs spirit and we tried to pass it on.

CHAPTER NINE

ELEGANCE PERSONIFIED OR A TOUCH OF TOSH

It may surprise a lot of people to know that Alan Gordon (or 'Tosh' as he was known) only played with Hibs for just on three years while he spent almost three times as long at Tynecastle. Yet it is as a Hibbie that he will be remembered.

Tosh was a key part of one of Hibs' greatest ever attacks, partnering Jimmy O'Rourke up front in Turnbull's Tornadoes. The pair complemented each other perfectly. Alan was tall and elegant, superb in the air and the small, dark buzz bomb Jimmy O'Rourke lapped up his lay-offs with predatory relish.

Like Tosh, many players have crossed the great divide between Gorgie and Easter Road, but few have done so successfully, especially after spending so long at Hearts. However there is no question where Alan's loyalty now lies. 'Whenever I was reporting at Tynecastle for radio or television in recent years Wallace Mercer would always make remarks about me being a Hibbie. I would have to say I was there as a neutral but he knew and I knew he knew I was green through and through. So there you are. Now you know, Wallace.

I grew up in a family that tended towards Hearts, but my experiences at Hibs and the way the fans treated me converted me totally. However I must admit to a moment of initial doubt the day I signed for Hibs. I was driving back along Queen Street and it struck me: 'What have I done?' Here I was, someone who had played for Hearts for eight years. Surely the fans would murder me? What's more I had always hated playing at Easter Road because of the slope. But how wrong I was. My Tynecastle past was never cast up to me and I settled in amazingly quickly. I even got used to playing on the slope.

My career had gone quiet you could say when Eddie Turnbull aproached Dundee United. Jim McLean had just taken over and I was keen to look after my accountant's career in

Edinburgh. As a youngster Rangers had tried to sign me before my debut for Hearts in 1961 against Celtic. At one stage Jock Stein tried to take me to Celtic with Willie Wallace but the deal fell through. I then had a spell in South Africa before coming back to Scotland and Dundee United. Eddie had been interested in taking me to Aberdeen and when he got the Hibs job I thought he might come in for me. So when the chance came in January 1972 I went for it. Jim McLean was graceful enough to admit later that Eddie had got the better deal that day. Jim was caretaking while Gerry Kerr stepped down and hadn't been made manager yet. I remember him saying after the deal had been made: 'I've a feeling I've just been fucking done.' I told him not to worry about it and not to think of going through with it as he was just an employee like me. But I suppose Jim was right as Eddie did get a bargain as I cost only £13,000.

My debut for Hibs wasn't a good omen as we lost 2–1 against Motherwell and Pat Stanton missed a penalty. As Pat strolled back past me he shook his head and said: 'I'm not to be trusted with penalties.' But it didn't take me long to appreciate what a good move I'd made. Over the years there has been a lot said about Eddie and his relationship with not just me but many other players. It's true we had words on a few occasions and I believe he broke up the League Cup winning team too early. And one of our run-ins has become a bit of Edinburgh football folklore. That's the time Eddie had had enough of me interrupting him with my point of view and told me: 'The trouble with you Gordon is that aw yer brains are in yer heid.' But a grudging and mutual respect existed until he unceremoniously got rid of me in December 1974 and had me training with the youngsters in the car park. However all that has never affected my opinion of him as a coach. He was second to none and that includes Jock Stein.

When I joined Eddie was putting together a great team that gelled in a very short time and it was the best I ever played in. As I've said, there was never anything said to me about my Hearts past and I quickly got into gear at Easter Road. It was not a problem as there were so many good players. I quickly realised what a coach Eddie Turnbull was. I was surprised at the tactics and training and how sophisticated it all was. In my estimation he was absolutely superb and I have never met anybody since who knew more about coaching and tactics.

I had my own approach as a player that I'd developed at

Eddie Turnbull's contribution to Hibs was second to none as a player and manager.
Here he is seen captaining a team against Vasco da Gama of Brazil.
(*Scotsman Publications*)

Lawrie Reilly had a better scoring record for Scotland than Law or Dalglish.
(*Scotsman Publications*)

Joe Baker. Ten years after . . . the Baker Boy returns to Easter Road.
(*Scotsman Publications*)

Gordon Smith was the greatest player to wear the green and white.
(*Scotsman Publications*)

RIGHT: *Eric Stevenson was rated international class by his colleagues.*
(*Scotsman Publications*)

BELOW LEFT: *Peter Cormack's class at Shankly's Liverpool proved he was not valued enough at Easter Road*
(*Scotsman Publications*)

BELOW RIGHT: *Jimmy O'Rourke: 'cut him and he'd bleed green.'*
(*Scotsman Publications*)

ABOVE: *Pat Stanton, 'The Quiet Man', says his bit at the 'Hands Off Hibs' rally in 1990.*
(*Scotsman Publications*)

LEFT: *Everything Alex Cropley did was magic.*
(*Scotsman Publications*)

ABOVE: *Jackie McNamara: only the Best was good enough for the man respected by all who played with him.*
(*Scotsman Publications*)

RIGHT: *For George Stewart a boyhood dream came true when Eddie Turnbull handed him the captain's armband.*
(*Scotsman Publications*)

ABOVE: *Testimony as to how highly Gordon Rae was regarded was evident when Manchester United led by Bryan Robson came to Easter Road.*

(*Scotsman Publications*)

LEFT: *Paul Kane: wholehearted for Hibs wherever he played.*

(*Scotsman Publications*)

ABOVE: *Mickey Weir. 'The Little Big Man' has always been the fans' favourite.*
(Murrie Thomson)

RIGHT: *Easter Road opened up the way to international honours for Darren Jackson.*
(Murrie Thomson)

Keith Wright immediately proved that he had the right stuff for Hibs as they won the Skol Cup.

(Scotsman Publications)

True grit at the back for ten years has caused Gordon Hunter no grievous bodily harm.

(Murrie Thomson)

Hearts, but Turnbull told me 'You're good at this and that but there are other things that can be improved.' And he went on to improve me as an individual player and I only wished that I had come under his guidance earlier in my career. His influence on the team was also second to none. He trained us very hard and asked a hell of a lot of us. Despite his reputation as a hard trainer, on match days he was so calm it was out of character. Today you see so many managers bawling and shouting from the touchline but Eddie knew all the hard work had to be done before the event. It was on the training ground that you became a good team and during the game he would watch like a hawk, picking up on things most people wouldn't see. His tactics talk before the game was short and sweet and it was the same again at half-time. He would come in and say I am going to tell you how to beat this team and he'd be right. As a result of Eddie's thorough preparation we knew exactly what we were going to do.

Of course I would always have something to say and gave my point of view. There was always mutual respect between us. Eddie could be a rough character and he was famous for his language, but he was very logical in explaining things and would put players in the right frame of mind. But remember Eddie also had an abundance of talent to work with.

Take John Brownlie at right back. The best there was in Scotland at that time. My dad would call me on a Friday night and want to know if Onion was playing. If he was he would come. It didn't matter whether I was playing or not. His leg break interrupted what could have been a fantastic career. I remember him playing for Scotland against Russia in Moscow and nutmegging their left winger before surging up the park and he was only 20 at the time. The rapport he established with Alex Edwards on the right was superb with great tip-tap football between them. Then all of sudden the play would be switched to Alex Cropley and Arthur Duncan on the left. Alex was so gifted and his touch allied to Arthur's speed was lethal. Our opponents never knew where we would come at them from we had so many options. I would stand up there at times doing bugger all, watching all this great football. And when the crosses came in we always knew what would happen. It was down to Eddie's tremendous routines during the week.

At the back there was the machine room where Jim Black and Sloop would graft away breaking down the opposition along with Pat Stanton playing in front of them. But everyone would be looking for every opportunity to attack. I was lucky to be stuck up there with these guys behind me. And of course there was Jimmy beside me. I don't really know how we formed such a good partnership – it wasn't something conscious. Jimmy could read instinctively my flicks and where they were going and he had that special talent – he was a natural goal scorer. Obviously Eddie had envisaged what the pair of us could do together and knew we would gell.

Everything seemed to come together so quickly and then we had a tremendous disappointment losing to Celtic in the 1972 Cup final. However we played Celtic four times in finals over an 18-month period and won three of them. But, if truth be told, the one we really wanted to win was the one we lost.

In the Cup final we were level 1–1 at half time with Billy McNeill and myself as goal-scorers. When Celtic got to 2–1 we should have levelled. Then John Brownlie mistimed a header back to Jim Herriot and Dixie Deans sneaked in and got a goal. We buckled after that at 3–1. Billy McNeill came in afterwards with the Cup and champagne and said we would like you guys to have a drink with us. It was the last thing we wanted but it was a nice gesture.

We got our chance of revenge with the Drybrough Cup in August winning 5–3 then came the League Cup final in December. It was a really hard game, but Pat Stanton was able to reciprocate taking the League Cup full of champagne round to the Celtic dressing-room and asking them if they'd like a drink. There was a geniunely good spirirt between the team with a lot of respect. I don't think there was a yellow card in either of those two games. They were two very good teams and it was unfortunate that we came along at a time when Celtic were so good.

I still feel that Hibs team could have achieved more than it did and we all thought Eddie should have left the 1972 team alone for another season or so and we could have done it. I think even he now might concede he was a bit premature. That team reached its peak in the short spell we had before being changed around at the end of 1972 and beginning of 1973 with the memorable New Year's game. Jimmy O'Rourke picked me up that morning as we went to meet the team in the North British Hotel. When I got in Jimmy said: 'What do you reckon?' I said 'Oh it could be one, two, three, four or five'. Well, it was 5–0 at half time and it could have been more. Hearts were unlucky that day but Hibs were hot.

Just before that both Jimmy and I had scored hat-tricks in an 8–1 win over Ayr and we had beaten Aberdeen 3–2 at Easter Road. I will always remember that game for a special goal. I knew when I saw Alex Cropley look up towards Arthur near the tunnel he would send him away. I was behind Alex that day and saw him raise his head and I took off. Alex chipped the ball down into the corner where the ground dips in at the corner of the North Stand. By now I was moving into the box and knew it would be coming over. When Arthur Duncan hit it even Arthur Duncan did not know where it was going. It came straight across like a rocket and I took a diving header sending it right through Bobby Clark's legs. I clearly remember the applause that day which is quite unusual as when I got up and ran back to the centre circle the crowd were still clapping because it was such a dynamic goal. I had known Alex Cropley was going to set Arthur Duncan up and Arthur had no first touch so it would be coming straight over. The surprise was that I had managed to get myself there in time. But credit must go to Arthur and it was he who crossed for the seventh goal at Tynecastle. I would watch from the middle and be ready to go. The quality and skill of the service was so good we had to score. In the 1972/73 season Arthur, Jimmy and I scored 99 goals. I got 43 in all competitions.

However, the '72/'73 season turned sour. I had got 27 goals in 26 games when we went to Yugoslavia for the return match with Hadjuk Split. I had scored a hat-trick in the 4–2 home win but we crashed 3–0 away and I picked up an injury. On returning from Yugoslavia we played Rangers at Ibrox and I didn't last the game. It was a bitter disappointment as I had been selected for Scotland to play England. I missed out on my chance to win a cap for my country and it is something I will always regret. Pulling on that navy blue jersey would have added the final touch to a marvellous season. But I did pick up an honour which doesn't fall to many players. I was chosen for the Rest of the World select to play Hamburg in the great German centre half and World Cup player Willie Schulz's testimonial game. Looking back it was some honour. Sixteen players were selected, among them Bobby Charlton, Florian Albert, Franz Beckenbauer, Carlos Alberto, Bobby Moore, Uwe Seeler, Denis Law, Leon Grabowski. Helmut Schoen was the manager and five would swap at half-time. I came on for Florian Albert and played up front with Gerd Muller.

Believe it or not, but at first Eddie Turnbull refused me permission to go but we had been put out of Europe so the club finally relented. It was a marvellous experience and we won 5–2. Willie Schulz had been the mainstay of the Hamburg defence a few years earlier at Easter Road when they'd beaten Hibs on the away-goals rule in the UEFA Cup in 1968. I still have the programme from the Rest of the World match as a memento and it is a small compensation for never winning a Scotland cap that at least I was good enough for a Rest of the World side. I was also involved in the squads for two Scotland games against Brazil and Switzerland but I never got the chance to show what I could do. I would have walked to Hampden for a Scotland jersey. Maybe if I had played for one of the Old Firm it would have been different. I was aware of it at Dundee United and it became clearer when I was at Hibs. I was also aware of it in journalism where there is a west coast bias in the media. This bias is even evident at youth level. It comes through at every level and Hampden has always been a second home to Rangers and Celtic. Don't tell me they would have won as many finals if Hampden was situated in Edinburgh or Dundee. It's a pity the football authorites have never thought of building an international stadium in central Scotland, near Stirling for example. However saying that I did enjoy playing at Hampden and scored on two occasions in finals against Celtic, the one that counted most being the last-minute winner in extra-time in the Drybrough final in 1974.

I also enjoyed playing at Parkhead and we had some classic clashes with Celtic. These were the great games in Scotland at that time. I never liked Ibrox, though, there was just something about the place. The old Ibrox pitch sloped away to the side like Rugby Park and Love Street, and Easter Road for that matter. Players like a flat surface so that you know the areas, distances, spaces etc on the pitch.

However, one of the great aspects of Eddie's side was how quickly we took to European football. We had a wonderful start in our two games against Sporting Lisbon and FC Besa. The Sporting Lisbon game in Portugal is considered by some as our finest display although we lost 2–1. That night we wore purple strips and it was a packed stadium. They were favourites to win the Cup Winners Cup but they knew we meant business when

Alex Cropley hit the post in the first minute. They went two-up getting both goals within a minute in the second half but Arthur Duncan pulled one back for us. It was important we never caved in to such a volatile atmosphere. There were about 100,000 at the game and they were favourites to win the trophy.

On the plane back I was sitting beside Gordon Smith and he gave us a tremendous compliment when he said this team would have wasted the Famous Five. The replay at Easter Road must go down as one of the top European games along with the famous Barcelona and Napoli games. I opened the scoring with a good header but Yazaldi levelled just on half-time. They were ahead again and we were chasing the game. Jim Herriot sent a long ball through and I went for it and won it when someone tackled me. I somehow rode it and managed to play the ball on, but fell on my face. I hadn't a clue where it had gone till I looked up to see Jimmy O'Rourke blasting it in. By now we knew we had them. Arthur was running riot on the wing and John Brownlie was surging forward and hit the post. I made it 3–1 with another header and Onion came up to me. He'd taken a knock and was a bit concussed. 'How do we stand?' he wanted to know. I told him it was 3–1 but he couldn't equate that with the away goals. So I said: 'Forget it. Just keep playing away and I will tell you after the game'. No matter how concussed he was he could finally understand we were through at 6–1.

In the next round against FC Besa it's not the 7–1 rout at Easter Road that's special for me but the 1–1 draw in Albania. I got the goal over there stabbing it in with my right foot. There's not many players that can say they've scored in Albania especially in those days. By now we really thought we could go all the way in the Cup Winners Cup but were caught out by Hadjuk Split. That and the way we tailed off in the league led Eddie to start tinkering with the side the next season.

In the Drybrough final we won against Celtic there were already new faces like Tony Higgins, Iain Munro and Des Bremner. A few weeks later we lost to Hearts 4–1 in the first derby since the 7–0 game. We'd played a League Cup tie in midweek and Eddie hammered us at training and then took us to Portobello baths for a session in the steam room. It was a classic example of Eddie driving us too hard at times and we were drained when we went out at Tynecastle. But the season picked up again. However, just after the New Year, Eddie signed Joe Harper. Joe Harper was a good player, but we didn't need him at that time. His first game was at Falkirk and Hibs substitutes were Gordon and O'Rourke. John Prentice told me later in the Falkirk dressing-room, they couldn't believe we weren't playing and it gave them a real lift. I always remember at the trackside watching Alex Edwards hitting over high balls which were drifting out for bye kicks. Now the team and our system had to be changed to accommodate Joe Harper.

Jimmy was to be sold to St Johnstone and within a year I was away to Dundee. Only later did I find out from Tommy Younger that Jock Stein had wanted to take me to Celtic, but Eddie refused and sold me to Dundee for a third of the fee. To be honest I would have been delighted to have gone to Celtic at that stage. Pat went there and had a couple of great seasons winning a league and cup medal. All he had to do, Stein said, was stand at the back and never cross the half-way line. I would have been happy to just stand up front and never come back.

Eddie was obviously doing what he felt was right in trying to build a new team and it is always easy to speak in hindsight. Now I don't bear any grudges – that was never my style and I have enjoyed bumping into him. We've even knocked a few golf balls around together. It was only after the event that I realised what a good team we were. We could have and maybe should have won the league and Cup. That team of ours was fed up beating Rangers during that period. After they had won the Cup Winners Cup they came to Easter Road at the start of the season in the Drybrough Cup semi-final and we thrashed them 3–0 and a few months later beat them in the League Cup semi-final. It was a coincidence that we ran into such a good Celtic side. Jock Stein was also a better man manager. He had a psychological edge on Eddie in that respect, but Turnbull was the better tactician. Eddie's failing was maybe that he was too gruff with players. But as I've always maintained he made me a better player and I would say the same applies to everyone who played under him.

As I look back on my career I appreciate that I played with and against truly great players. I made my professional debut playing alongside Willie Bauld and played against Gordon Smith when he was with Dundee and Jim Baxter at Rangers. The most complete opponent I came up against was Kenny Dalglish. He had everything.

Although my great partnership at Hibs was with Jimmy O'Rourke a lot of people may not remember that I started at

Hibs playing alongside Joe Baker. Joe was at the tail end of his career in his second spell with the club. However players always recognise the talent of others and Joe was an incredible player. I remember watching him annihilating Billy Wright when Hibs played Wolves back in the '50s. Joe was not the same player as he had been but I was still surprised how quick he was. The first goal I scored for Hibs was playing up front with Joe against Airdrie in the Cup. I headed one in off the post and then headed down for Joe to score in the ninetieth minute and the fans came piling onto the pitch.

Taking into consideration my great spell with Hibs it amazes me to think I actually spent only two years eleven months at the club. So much seemed to happen in such a short spell. My career finished a year later against Hearts when Jim Jefferies broke a bone in my foot. I was only 30, but as big George Stewart said to me: 'You've finished where you started.' Maybe so but the days I'll always really remember are the ones at Easter Road.

CHAPTER TEN

THE SODJER'S TALE

To have a football team named after you says it all, but to how many players has that happened? Not to Pele, Maradona as far as we know nor Kenny Garland for that matter. But that honour was bestowed upon one of Turnbull's Tornadoes.

Alex Cropley was such a hit in the early '70s the Liberton team asked him to honour them by granting permission for them to use his name. Crops had that effect on people. Maybe it was because he looked so young and frail yet he was as hard as nails and had wonderful skill.

Easter Road was surely the only outcome for the Magdalene lad whose schooldays were spent in the shadow of the North stand at Norton Park.

When I went there we used to regularly see the Hibs players after training and looked up to them. While I played on Saturdays it was a big thing to go to see Hibs in European matches. But we were a bit starstruck by players like Davie Gibson, Willie Hamilton, Neil Martin, Alex Scott and Eric Stevenson. But Willie was the main man. He was unlucky he didn't achieve more in the game and get greater recognition at international level.

I went on to the ground staff at Easter Road at the same time as John Brownlie and Willie McEwan and at the same time played for Edina Hibs where the three of us were in a very good under-17 side. I hadn't really thought about turning pro and was looking for a trade. My father, who had played for Aldershot, thought this was the best idea. It was Bob Shankly who was the manager at that stage, but when Willie McFarlane took over he persuaded me to go full time and my debut came in a 1–0 win over St Mirren when Eric Stevenson was injured. Eric was really good to me in those days, helping me to settle in and giving me a lot of encouragement. I was a bit in awe of them all.

It was when Peter was transferred to Nottingham Forest that my real chance came and I took his place. Not long after Willie McFarlane got the sack and Eddie Turnbull arrived. And that was the point when I really learned to play football. He was a great coach and he made you aware of everything, every department of the game in his usual nice manner. I got on as well with Eddie as anybody else did at the time. But I get on better with him today and whenever I see him we have a great chat. What I achieved in later years in the game was all down to him. He put seeds into my mind that fertilised later on into what football was all about. I had the basics already but he helped me develop them and use them in the best way. He pointed out to me where to stand and why I should take up that position, when to make a run, when I should look for this man etc. It was like going back to school.

Eddie could not be other than the way he was. There were no kids gloves. We were all treated the same and in truth he wasn't a man manager. I know some didn't like him, but I can never forget what he did for me. He was the first real manager I had, and I have always been a great believer that you should take as many bollockings going if you are getting a win bonus.

When I had first played for Hibs I was put out on the wing as they considered me so slight that I couldn't play anywhere else, but Eddie soon had me in the middle. My slightness was deceptive. I was a hard player and my dad had always told me to go in hard as that way you are less likely ever to get hurt, and I was quite proud people used to say about me that, pound for pound, I was one of the best tacklers going. Any of the injuries I picked up were never a result of my going into tackles. There was one time early on in my career when John Greig and I both steamed into a tackle. It was John who came out worse with a broken foot. I never minded playing against John as you always knew where you stood with him. He would kick you from the front.

Looking back on it all everything happened for me at an early age. I was playing in a side that wanted to play football, full of great players and with a manager who knew more about football than anyone else. I was also lucky that I was a home town boy. That makes things easier. People know you already and you get that bit of recognition and people wanted me to do well. I just took it all for granted at the time. It was all a bit of a rollercoaster at the time and I wish now I had been able to stand back and take more in. By the time I got my first cap I was so delighted if I was chocolate I would have eaten myself!

Mind you Eddie at one stage said to me that things were coming on too quickly and too easily and I wasn't playing particularly well. Whether he meant it or not I'm not sure as I think he was just trying to give me a bit of balance. But things went so well for me in such a short time. After only 18 months under Eddie I had won two caps. I was first picked along with Bob Wilson by Tommy Docherty. Both of us were born in England although I had grown up in Scotland unlike Bob. It was a bit of a gimmick by the Doc and he got the papers on our side. The first game was against Portugal and was a good one and I played very well. I was surprised myself how easily I slotted into international football and I think I surprised a few other people as well. The next international I was not so lucky as I broke a bone in my foot and Kenny Dalglish made his debut, coming on as substitute. And that was the end of my international career. I did have a good chance of going to Argentina in 1978 when I was playing down south but I broke my leg and just had to accept it as a fact of life. When I got picked for Scotland I was struck by the Anglos like Billy Bremner, George Graham, Eddie Gray and John O'Hare. They were all very professional and could teach the home-based players a lesson about the game. I must admit I was a bit starry eyed over this.

That whole period was such a good spell. Hibs were doing well in the Cup Winners Cup, on our way to the League Cup and were on form in the league.

We reached our peak on New Year's Day when we beat Hearts 7–0. Some of the players like Pat and Jimmy, the real Hibbies in the team, were delirious. My family were out in force at the game and I think I went out that night with a few of the team. My attitude to derbies was just that I wanted to do well. I rarely lost one. The goal I scored in the 7–0 game was laid out for me on a plate. I got the ball from Alan Anderson. It seemed to take so long for the ball to land for me and I just let loose with a left-footed volley. I scored a few good ones in derbies. One of the most memorable was that one from near the byeline up the slope at Easter Road when I got both in a 2–0 win. I only saw it again on the television not so long ago.

When we beat Hearts 7–0 the score could easily have been 10–2. We were playing some excellent football, but I don't think we realised how good we were at the time. Eddie Turnbull actually said to us around that time that we were probably better than the Famous Five as a team which was saying something coming from Eddie. It was the only compliment he ever gave us. But it must have been a bit of a brainstorm as he was back to his usual the next day. It was a pity because that was Eddie's only failing as a manager. He couldn't really talk to us. That was the difference between him and Jock Stein. Stein could get someone off the street and put a Celtic strip on his back and he would be a world beater.

We had some classic battles with Celtic. They were some team in those days and many of their team had been in the European Cup winning side. We played really well when we beat them in the League Cup final and our goals were well worked. It was particularly good as it was not so long before that they had leathered us in the Cup.

We had the football to beat Celtic although they were an unbelievable team, but for some reason during that period they had an edge on us. I don't know what it was but they always seemed to raise their game against us and play out of their skins. Maybe it was because in some ways we were similar – both really good footballing sides. I think if we had come up against any other team it would not have been such a problem. Our own team had a lot of character in it, Jim Herriot was an ex-international and like the best was a bit mad. He would blacken his eyes to cut out the glare of the sun and sometimes liked to go for a wee wander out of his box. John Brownlie was the best full back in Scotland and Erich Schaedler had unbelievable strength. Erich helped make me the player I was because he was so quick and I knew that I could leave a man and he would take two. Sloop and Cilla were a good balance in the middle and wee Alex Edwards was one of the finest kickers of the ball I have ever seen. His only problem was his temperament. Pat Stanton played in between us and he was immense in midfield but he was better as a centre half. That shows how good he was. Not many people appreciated he was world class at the back. But he was a poor captain as he was too quiet. Jimmy and Alan were a good combination up front with Alan flicking on a lot for Jimmy and then there was Flyer on the wing.

We had great times abroad and some of our games were classics. One of the most memorable, but not for the football, was the trip to Albania. It was cut off from the world in those days and when I say it was poor I am talking poor. When Besa were in Edinburgh you ought to have seen them attack the buffet after the game and get stuck into the whisky. They thought it was so lavish. We took our own cook over for the second leg and were stuck in a big 1940s hotel. But for some reason they took it as an insult that we wanted to cook our own food and served up meat red raw. The actual ground was like a school pitch and the seats in it were occupied by Chinese officials. It was something else and before the game Mr Kerr, the director, who was a plumber was fixing the cludgies for us in the dressing-room . When Besa came out in their cherry red strips they had painted their numbers on the back.

The thought was at the back of our minds that we might never get out of the place as there were fighter planes on the airfield by our plane making sure we left only on their say-so. And there was a big tanker that had siphoned off the fuel so we couldn't leave until they said we could go. When we arrived there had been a couple of soldiers standing there like something out of Doctor Zhivago with ancient rifles and I'd swear they hadn't moved when we were leaving two days later. But despite all the differences the crowd was as fanatical about football as you'd get anywhere.

But it was some contrast to other places we'd stayed in. Against Sporting Lisbon we stayed in the hotel at Estoril that had been used in the latest 007 movie. Juventus was another highlight. Their training pitch was like Wembley. They were an excellent side and Altafini was some player although he didn't look it. He was old, balding and pudgy with greased-back hair, but he could get away from you. In Italy during a lull in the game there was a huge roar as if a goal had been scored. We didn't realise what was happening but it was Altafini. He'd got up off the bench to warm up to come on. He changed the game at Easter Road when he came on. We had been winning 2–1 after I had put us ahead, but then Altafini arrived and he got two goals out of nothing.

The night we played Sporting at Easter Road was an outstanding performance. Alan Gordon, Jimmy and Arthur ran riot that night. One of their Brazilians raked Sloop with six studs in a tackle, and was smart enough to drift over to where I was sharpish. Sloop couldn't afford to go after him so he said to me 'Get him, sodjer.' I wandered over and told the guy. 'I'm going to do you.' He must have understood because he told me to 'fuck off'. I got the fright of my life. I never thought he understood English.

Another great European tie was the Leeds game. Hibs took a great support to Elland Road and it was a great surface we played on that night. We should have won and I remember setting up big Tony for a header when he jumped down instead of up. He was one of the few players who could do that. At Easter Road we played well but their keeper had a blinder, but the real difference that night was Billy Bremner. It was the best display by a sweeper I have ever seen. It went to penalties and Pat missed the first one. I had to take the second and scored and it went right to the last kick. Before the tie there had been some talk from their camp they were not too concerned as they wanted to win the English league. But they were over the moon when they won and Revie was on the pitch hugging Bremner. He'd also been on before the penalties, coaching them, which was illegal. It just showed how much it mattered to them. Tom Hart appealed against it but the result stood.

These were all great evenings and Eddie would have us as prepared as you can be even down to what sort of playing surface it was. In league and Cup games against slow teams like Rangers and Airdrie he'd get the grass cut really short so the ball would zoom across the ground really quickly.

Gradually that team was breaking up and then came my move to Arsenal. I had been getting tapped by Arsenal for over a year and their scout had come to see me at my house but I told him to contact Eddie Turnbull. Chelsea came in as well and Eddie told me to go and see the chairman as Dave Sexton was coming up. Sexton wanted a quick answer as Chelsea were going on tour to Australia. I phoned Arsenal to let them know the situation as I reckoned Hibs were set on selling me by now. They had bought Ally McLeod from Southampton and I was told I was their only asset and the club needed the money. We were out training at Hunters Hall when John Fraser came over and told me the manager wanted to see me. Eddie was straight to the point. 'We can see you don't want to play for Hibs and Arsenal have come in. You can speak to them.' I was sent back to Easter Road and before I knew it was on the plane to Heathrow and that was it.

I had told Eddie Turnbull that all I wanted at Easter Road was what everyone else was getting and I would be happy to stay. I didn't want to leave but the club were not budging. However I am now glad that I did leave. The money made a big difference. Straightaway I got a 100 per cent rise and Arsenal were a really big club. I was also playing in front of big crowds every week and a better standard of teams. I feel I improved as a player as well even when I went to Villa, a side which played similarly to Hibs at that time. Des Bremner followed me to Villa a few years later and was in their European Cup winning side. When Des first broke through at Hibs as a right back I didn't fancy him much. He was after all following in John Brownlie's footsteps, but when he moved into midfield he did very well.

It was interesting to note the different styles of the managers. Eddie would always be first into the dressing–room after a game and give you a slap on the back if you had won. If you lost the door would come off its hinges. But one thing you were guaranteed was a great team talk from Eddie. Bertie Mee at Arsenal was so different. A real gent, he would leave all the work on the pitch to the coaches.

Looking back on my career now there is nothing I really regret but I do wish I had known how good I was. As a laddie I would have played for nothing and it was an honour going out in those lovely green and white strips for Hibs. I took it all very seriously and hated losing but it all just raced along. It is only when you pack it in and people now compare you to past and present teams and players that you realise your own worth. And what people say to me now I wish I had been told then. Maybe at the time they thought it might go to my head and I might have been a lesser player but I don't know. Confidence is such a key to being a good player and it should always be encouraged in youngsters. But I do appreciate that I was very fortunate to play with the guys I did, and against those like Bremner, Eusebio and, in Scotland, Bobby Murdoch. It was a privilege to be on the park with them. But today I have to admit a lot of the football doesn't impress me. I'm sorry to say that but in our team everyone could trap and pass a ball. I find it difficult nowadays watching teams with a few players who can't really do that.

Times change and so does football and every generation looks back. I remember once asking Tam Preston and Paddy Buckley how many of our team would have got in to the Famous Five's side. Paddy didn't mess about: 'You wouldn't even have made it as a hamper boy.'

I don't know whether it was the drink talking or the truth.

I remember that when Bobby Charlton packed it in as a player he said his love for the game had gone. I can't understand that. How can you stop loving the game? I decided to call it a day when players started to go past me who could not have laced my boots a few years earlier. My cartilage trouble had taken its toll.

I still like to contribute to the game at any level and coach a team. It would also be nice to have the opportunity to contribute something to Hibs but whether there is a place for old players is another matter.

Alex was a guest of honour at Liberton Cropley's 20th anniversary dinner.

It's a shame about their recent troubles, but I was honoured when they asked me all these years ago if I would mind them calling themselves 'Cropley'. I had moved to Arsenal and received a letter from Eddie Campbell. I knew Eddie from back when we won the League Cup. That night as I came out of the Balmoral, the NB in those days, Eddie was waiting and asked me to autograph his body. So I signed his arm. That was my first connection with Liberton Cropley.

But it is things like that, the relationship with the fans and the great times I had with players at Hibs, that are the important things about football that really count.

CHAPTER ELEVEN

THE LEADER OF THE BAND

It would be impossible to fill Pat Stanton's place in the hearts of Hibs fans, but there was probably no one who could have done a better job replacing the 'Quiet Man' than Jackie McNamara. It says so much about McNamara the man that he became such a favourite at Easter Road, admired by fans and fellow professionals. And even Pat says Hibs got the best of the deal when the Stanton-McNamara switch took place as Jackie was an outstanding servant for over a decade while Pat just had another season left in him. However it was not all plain sailing for Jackie Mac and he remembers the stick he took at first.

It was quite a while before I was accepted and to be truthful I did not play too well at first. But I was playing as a right back. The North Stand used to give me some abuse and as any player in Scotland will tell you they can really dish it out. If you can survive that you can survive anything. It was only really when I switched to sweeper that the fans really accepted me.

It was at the start of the 1976/77 season when I saw Pat coming into Parkhead when Celtic were playing Dundee United. I wondered what Pat was doing there and then when Jock Stein put the deal to me I was prepared to accept it.

Jackie the Red as he came to be known is happy to scotch rumours that Celtic got rid of him because he was a communist.

I have heard that nonsense that Celtic got rid of me because of politics, but that is rubbish. My father was a Red Clydesider and I am proud of that. I am still a left-winger and will never cover that up and that's despite going to work for a stockbrokers when I left school.

I had signed for Celtic as a goal-scoring inside forward but my career had reached a low point. I had a cruciate knee ligament injury, a bit like Ian Durrant's but not as bad. Celtic were open to offers for me. Jock Stein had phoned me up wanting me to do a swop with Partick for Bobby Houston and I will always be grateful to Alan Hansen for warning me off. I was not really grateful enough until I had the experience of finding out how bad Bertie Auld really was when he became manager at Hibs.

Jock Stein then came back to me for a swap with Pat but warned me that if I let the papers know it would blow up in my face. Of course, I was delighted and Hibs were a full-time team unlike Partick. The only thing Hibs never checked out were my teeth. The medical was like something out of Alex Haley's *Roots*, the going over Eddie Turnbull gave me to see I was the right goods. Looking back on it the deal worked out well for both Pat and me. Pat won a league and Cup medal with Celtic and if he had played there earlier he would have won 100 caps.

Working under Eddie Turnbull was some experience. He was the best manager I have had and that includes Stein, Ormond and Auld. He may have been deficient in man-management but he opened up the game for me and how to play it. He would put you in all sorts of situations and he gave me so much confidence. Jock Stein was lucky as he had marvellous players at Celtic, better resources than Eddie Turnbull. Having played for both, all I can say is Eddie was exceptional and Jock's record speaks for itself.

But my first five months at Hibs were not too good. I was played at right back and got booed off regularly. But Eddie stuck with me. Then after five months he sold John Blackley and moved me in as sweeper. My first game there was against Aberdeen and we drew 0–0. I was up against Joe Harper who had gone back to Aberdeen and I never let him get a kick at the ball. I think that's what won the North Stand over. From then on I made the position mine. Eddie had helped me but I had helped him because he had sold a legend.

Turnbull was some man and at that stage he was building a new team with the likes of Bobby Smith and Tony Higgins. Tam McNiven was a good trainer, but he was a timid man and Turnbull would bully him as he did the players but I could always stick up for myself. The biggest disappointment for that team was when we lost the Cup final against Rangers in 1979. We should have won it in the first game and I only remember too well Colin Campbell being brought down by Peter McCloy with three minutes to go. I've still got the video and I tell you it was a penalty. But the highlight of that Cup run was the quarter-final tie against Hearts. I loved it when my big pal George Stewart got the winner. As everyone knows George is a red hot Hibbie and scoring against Hearts could not have meant more to any player. It was only at the end of my career that we started to lose against Hearts, but most of my time at Easter Road we rolled them over regularly. It's not like it has been in recent times but I can see the tide turning again with three wins for Hibs last season.

I always enjoyed the derbies and it meant a lot to me not to let down the Hibs community. The derby is the worst game of all to lose as you let down so many people, but there was never any of the hatred you get attached to Old Firm derbies.

Although Hibs slipped in the '80s our team in the late '70s had a lot of class players. Big George was an enormously important part of the team at the end of his career and playing with him was a great pleasure. Not many would get past the pair of us. It might surprise people to know that George could be a bit of an introvert on the park and at times maybe lacked a wee bit confidence, but he would take it as a personal affront if somebody scored against him. One season we only got 18 goals scored against us in the Premier Division.

It was also at that time I teamed up with my pal Ralph Callachan and we have been great friends ever since. Ralph sometimes got a bit of stick for being an ex-Hearts player but a guy like Ralph could handle that no bother. He'd just laugh about it. It's the sort of thing that could have got to a lesser man.

Definitely the best player at Easter Road at that time was Ally McLeod. Ally was a really skilful player and never really got the recognition he deserved. A lot of people would think he was lazy but the players knew what Ally was doing and he was forever up and down the park and never hiding. He may not have been the greatest runner but when you had a player like Des Bremner who had an engine and a half you did not have to worry. But when Des left for Aston Villa the team missed him and it was one of the components that led to our relegation. But even as George and I got older Hibs had good young central defenders in Gordon Rae and Craig Paterson who was a very good player. However, for me, Big George was the best at the back. But I'll always remember a young man making a mark on me, literally. He was only 15 at the time and launched in to tackle me in sandshoes. It was like a collision in a Tom and Jerry cartoon. It was the young Gordon Hunter and I thought 'He'll do for me'. He broke into the Hibs team as a 17-year-old and has been there ever since. At present he and Steven Tweed can build a great partnership together. I've known Tweedie since he was 10 and have watched him develop. I wish George could get him for a couple of hours and teach him how to go through the ball and fully use his physique. I think he has great potential and could become captain of Scotland one day.

Gordon Hunter was just one of a wee group on the ground staff who all had a lot of potential. Wee Mickey's career in some ways has been a disappointment as he has so much skill. Another youngster coming through was Kano. He was some boy and he still owes me a lot of dosh. He's a player who contributed a lot to Hibs over the years.

It's also been good to see these guys back in Europe as we were the last Hibs team for over a decade to do so. In the first round we were on dodgy ground after only beating Norkopping 3–2 at home and knew we would be struggling in Sweden but George and I played out of our skins that night and we drew 0–0. I was suspended for the Sochaux game and we went out in the next round to Strasbourg. In that game I had a wee set-to with Ally McLeod. In European football the back men get a lot of the ball and Ally was not pleased about the service he was getting from us. He could be very critical. What made it worse was that he was an articulate, bright, lad with a really acid tongue. Going up the tunnel he started calling me for everything and we had a wee set-to. When we got into the dressing-room he was still going at it so I leathered the ball and got him full in the face. Quick as flash he said 'That's the first time you've caught me with the ball all night.' Just as well big Tony Higgins was there to stop me as I went for him.

We had a few characters at the club at that time and things got livelier when George Best arrived. It was unbelievable the interest he generated. In the first home game against Partick where you might be expecting 5000 over 21,000 turned up. He was a marvellous guy and everyone really liked him. The press interest was incredible and there's the famous story about the picture of George and all the pints. There were journalists in the pub and one of them offered George a £500 cheque for a picture, but he just ripped it up. But they got their photo anyway with all the glasses which were already on the table around George.

As I said he was a lovely guy and did me the honour of coming up for my testimonial game against Newcastle a couple of years later.

As we slid closer to relegation that season we were due to play Rangers at Ibrox. Peter Cormack was back at Hibs for a short while and was playing and so was George, but there was no sign of him. Willie Ormond was by now Turnbull's assistant and he read out the team and the subs were McNamara and Higgins. I was only sub three times at Hibs. Once because I was carrying an injury, another time at the beginning of my career, but this was the low point. Anyway George had still not arrived and Peter's knee was swollen up like a balloon. Tony starts to strip and says to Willie: 'What's up with George?' Wee Willie replied: 'Oh aye, aye he's getting a wee jag from the doc because of the drink.' Then Eddie Turnbull walked in and says: 'George has a rash, he's got a wee virus.' Big Tony turns round in front of everybody and says: 'Heh, Willie, I thought you told us he was getting a wee jag for the bevvy.' Willie didn't know where to look but Tony wasn't finished as he shouted over to me.

'McNamara, you and me must be some players if we can't get a game and a cripple and a drunk get in before us.'

But worse lay ahead for me with the arrival of Bertie Auld. I had remembered Alan Hansen's warning and it certainly came to fruition. Not long after he'd arrived we were training at Hunters Hall. Eddie Turnbull had always encouraged me to move up and be an extra man in midfield. Well, in this practice game I broke through in front of Craig Paterson when all I heard was 'Fucking stap the game.' Bertie Auld came over.

'You are my valve. You don't go in front of my centre half.' So we started up again. Another chance came and I moved forward. It was automatic as Eddie had coached me so well to exploit the opportunity when you had the ball. It almost came as second nature.'Fuckin stap the game.' This time he was over, right in my face. 'Who do you think you are some fucking prima donna superstar? Get aff the pitch.' So he told me to walk back to Easter Road about three miles away. I wandered over to the dressing-room and was ready to break the door down. Alan Hart drew up and wondered what I was doing. I told him I had had a fall out with the manager so he offered me a lift back to Easter Road. The lads told me later they weren't allowed onto the bus back until Bertie had searched under all the seats to make sure I didn't get a lift back. When they got back Tam McNiven started calling out the wage slips. 'Miller, Paterson, Rae, Rodier.' When I asked where mine were he told me the manager wanted to see me. I went up the stairs and Bertie wanted to shake my hand for standing up to him but I refused. Then he had me back in the afternoon. Just me, him, and five other staff teaching me to lay and lift into the hole as he called it. I had been a pro for nine years and basically he was now try-ing to teach me just to hump the ball as far up the park as pos-sible. I held my tongue and just tried to do my best for the team. This went on for a while, but I was sure he was going to get me down. Tom Hart called me to speak about a testimonial. He liked me and I appreciated what they were offering me, but I told Tom about my situation and that one thing for sure was I would be at Easter Road longer than Bertie. Not long after that he was out. The day we heard at training that Pat Stanton was coming was like a breath of fresh air. Jim McArthur, who was not the most athletic of players, started doing cartwheels when we heard the news and the players started singing 'Happy Days are Here Again'.

Which they were with Pat, but unfortunately he did not get the backing he needed. If he had things could have been differ-ent. That has been something that has helped Alex Miller a lot; he has a good board behind him. But I don't think the punters realised the circumstances Pat was working in. However, Pat made some signing getting Roughie. He was so laid back you'd think he was dead half the time. But what a keeper!

However things are going well at Hibs again. What has happened has been marvellous for Alex Miller. When the *Evening News* did their phone in asking 'Do you want this man sacked?' it made me sick. His job was being put on the line by this pressure and I was delighted when he went out and won his next game. I know he has had his critics and as a fan I have felt disappointed by his tactics at times, but you have to give it to him – he is meticulous and one of the hardest workers in foot-ball. What's more he has won a trophy and who was the last manager to do that? So overall you have to say he has done a great job.

It's good to see Hibs on the up again. When I was a player the club was slipping but now it is far better organised. One of the highlights for me was the day we were promoted back to the Premier Division. It was important because Hibs need to be at the forefront of Scottish football. But on a personal level I'll never forget the day I won over the North Stand and they started chanting my name.

CHAPTER TWELVE

BIG DODE

If ever there was a Hibs player who wore his heart on his sleeve more than Jimmy O'Rourke it was George Stewart. The main difference was that while nearly all of Jimmy's career was in the green and white George only got the chance at the tail end of his career. But the long wait was obviously worth it.

The most memorable thing that ever happened to me at Easter Road was when Turnbull threw me the ball and said 'Big man, you're now the captain.' It was the biggest thrill of my life.

It gave me great pride to walk out as Hibs captain whether we were at Easter Road or away, but the pinnacle was doing so at Hampden in a Cup final. I was so proud and really honoured. If you are a Hibs man, it's the ultimate. But there's another side to it as well. If you are a Hibs man it puts extra pressure on you. You feel you can't let anybody down. You are playing for your mates, your family. I never felt that pressure in all my time at Dundee. I was there as a professional, but don't get me wrong, I always gave everything I had. But it was a job.

When I came to Hibs I was 28 and I felt pressure I had never before had in my life. At Dundee I had played in big matches and in Europe against the like of AC Milan. I spoke to Pat about it. He had had a lot of years as a youngster growing up at Easter Road and been able to get used to it, but he appreciated what I felt. When the chance came to play for Hibs – which to be honest I had given up all hope of – it was a football dream come true. Eddie Turnbull bought me and I'll always be grateful to him for that. You've got to remember Eddie was just Eddie. Some players found him hard to live with but I always got on fine with him. When Eddie had had a few bevvies he used to say: 'Ach son, you were never a player until I signed you.' 'Well, I did cost you £60,000,' I'd say, which was a fair amount of money in those days.

Eddie would ignore that. 'If I had had you earlier you would have played for Scotland.' That was Eddie for you.

One thing for sure was he was by far the best manager I had ever had. The way he handled the game, read it and coached it was second to none. Just listening to the way he talked about football you could tell he was the best.

Although Hibs were not the club they had been in Eddie's early years when I joined them we still had a lot of good times and came as a close to winning the Cup as any Hibs team since 1902. We also played in Europe and also used to beat Hearts all the time. Probably the game that stands out most from those years at Easter Road was when we beat Hearts in the Cup in 1979. It's amazing how rarely the clubs have met in the Cup and the last time Hibs had played them was in 1971 when Arthur got the winner in a 2–1 win at Tynecastle. Arthur was still in the team in 1979. I'd love to say the Cup final that year was the most memorable but we lost it. Although we played exceptionally well at times we never had the right players up front to do it. Defensively we were sound with McNamara, myself and Dessie Bremner and there were some really skilful players like Ally McLeod but we were only half a team. Rangers themselves were not too clever at that time. Celtic had beaten them for the league title and they were there for the beating. We could have had them in both the 0–0 games. And in the third we went into extra time 2–2. Then with a minute or so to go Arthur headed into our own net. I saw it going over and thought it was going out until I turned round and saw it in the back of the net. Arthur was crying and we kicked off but that was it.

It was the longest Cup final ever in Scottish football and finally finished on 29 May. Then we had to meet them again in the league and beat them at Easter Road. They talk about too many games nowadays but we were still playing into June. Imagine anyone playing three Cup finals nowadays. In the quarter-final against Hearts I was captain and won the toss so chose to shoot up the slope. Halfway through the first half Ralph Callachan took a corner and I went up for it. I remember Derek O'Connor went with me and Jim Jefferies but I beat them to it and headed it in. We'd gone into the game thinking we would win and pushed for a second before half-time but it never came. Just at the start of the second half big Gordon Rae raked one in from about 30 yards. I think they scored with about two minutes to go but by then we were thinking about getting the cigars out and going to the 'Jinglin Geordie' for a few bevvies.

That was our local during the week, but then again it may have been 'Leerie's' in Dublin Street as that's where we often went on a Saturday. It's funny thinking about it today as players aren't supposed to hang out in pubs. Turnbull knew where we went but he knew we trained extremely hard. Turnbull was famous for his training methods and what he put into them. Jim McLean, who's a friend of mine from my Dundee days, used to be on the phone to me all the time when I went to Hibs: 'What has Eddie been giving you for training?' Jim idolised Eddie. He thought he was the best. I think Jim based a lot of his mannerism and everything else on Eddie, the rough with the smooth. After a brutal session Turnbull would say 'Away and have a couple of pints you've worked hard.' He knew we were professional enough not to get blootered on the night before a game. Nobody ever abused it. Well, on second thoughts I take that back as there was George Best. There is an exception to everything. But George was a brilliant guy and everyone who was at Hibs at that time would back that up.

I well remember the time he got caught by a photographer in the 'Jinglin'. There was a table that a group of press boys had just left and seven or eight of us moved in and sat down. You know what it was like if journalists had been at it, empty glasses everywhere. No one had cleared their pints away while Ally McLeod was up at the bar getting in the first round when this boy pops up and takes a photo. We never thought about it, but the boy had obviously been lying in wait. George just shook his head and apologised to us saying he hoped we wouldn't get in trouble for it.

But we told Turnbull the truth of the matter when the picture appeared all over the papers and that the boy had set the photo up. None of us had even had a drink yet. To be fair if the boy had come back four hours later he might have got a genuine photo but he didn't.

Best was a different class of guy despite all the hassle he had to put up with. I had a lot of time for him. He was a really good lad and never acted the superstar. His move to Easter Road as far as I was concerned was a great thing. It aroused great interest in Hibs which could only be a good thing. Mind you Ally McLeod was not pleased when he heard George was getting two grand a game. Ally was very upset. He got on to Jackie the

Red about it and the pair of them said to me 'You go and get it sorted out, George'. I told them that I was only the captain of the football team not the chairman. What could I do? Anyway I had a word and Turnbull said: 'Away you go. That Jackie the Red and that McLeod are winding you up about Best's wages.' I said 'Oh no, boss, just raising a point.' Anyway it was a losing battle so I just left it.

Life was never dull when George was around. When we played Ayr United in the Cup the match was on a Sunday. As I was captain I always came a bit early to the North British for the pre-match meal. The French rugby team were staying there and had won the Grand Slam the day before. Anyway I walked in and who should I see coming round a corner but John Fraser and John Lambie carrying the boy Best. He was legless. Turnbull came chasing round after them and spotted me. 'Come here, you' he growled. 'What is it boss?' 'Now whatever you do don't tell anybody what you've seen.' 'Dinnae worry about that, but I'll tell you what when he doesn't turn up for the pre-match meal there'll be questions.'

What had happened was that the French boys had invited the bold boy Best to join their celebrations the night before. So Champagne Charlie joined in the fun that lasted all night. So by now he was out the box. Even a player like George couldn't have played that day, the state he was in.

We had a lot of fun and games with George . . . but above all he was a great guy and I shudder to think what sort of player he was when he was younger and sober. When he was up here he was 32 to 33, but he could still be dynamite. He must have been marvellous in his hey-day. Pele got it right when he said George was the best.

The funny thing was that George was a good trainer – when he turned up. When he didn't, you just put two and two together. You'd marvel at the things he could do with the ball in training and he was good with the young guys. But we got a laugh watching George trying the one-twos with Benny. George once said to me: 'George, does that boy Benny Brazil think a lay-off is a week in his bed?' George was not trying to be disre-spectful he just did not understand how he was getting a game.

The funny thing is I don't know if George played in a derby because Hearts were relegated that season. But not that we needed him. In those days it was just a matter of turning up. I used to hand my wife a right few quid and tell her to get a washing machine. You knew your £250 derby bonus was a dead cert. That attitude was inbred in us. I think in my time at Hibs, Hearts won just once. As a Hibs player or supporter going to play the Hearts you had no complex. There was none of this 21 games without a win nonsense. Take the Cup game for instance, when I scored I never thought for a minute we were not going to win.

That day Turnbull just did his usual. He told us how we were going to go out and play. He never spoke about the other team. I liked that attitude. It was positive. Let's worry about us not them. Turnbull didn't give two hoots whether it was Europe or a Cup final. I think too many managers today get wrapped up in that.

I was lucky as well playing alongside Jackie. We had a really good partnership and were room-mates on trips abroad. Probably we were too late in getting together. I was quite old and Jackie played on after me. I played with a few like Blackley but Jackie was the best for me. Big Gordon Rae also went on to do a good job at the back. When I went back when Pat was manager Gordon was still a centre forward. I said 'Let's try him at the back'. It took him time to adjust. He had a few nightmares, but he made the position his own and ended up with a testimonial from Hibs. I have a lot of good memories of that spell working with Pat as manager. It was not all doom and gloom although we didn't have two pennies to rub together. People don't realise how skint the club was. You wouldn't believe the way things were run then. But we did bring through a group of young players that were to stand the club in good stead. Take a look at them today – Mickey Weir, Gordon Hunter, Calum Milne, Willie Miller, John Collins, Eddie May, Kevin McKee. Kano had already been signed by Bertie Auld. We had no youth policy and no money. But they came through and I would like to think we set Hibs up well for the future. Alan Rough was our one big buy and he said in his own book that the happiest time in his career was at Easter Road. We were Hibs people and our philosophy was that players must enjoy themselves. If they didn't make it or moved elsewhere we wanted them to look back on it it as a good period in their career.

Pat was the most educated guy I have ever worked with when it came to knowing about the game. He is a big loss to it. His knowledge surpasses anyone else I know. Jimmy was the best I have ever seen with kids 16 or 17 years old. One of my best memories is of the time we went to Tannadice. It was the year they won the Premier League with Narey, Hegarty, Sturrock and co. I said to Pat that we should play with five forwards because they thought we would come up to defend. Somebody said we didn't have five fucking forwards. I insisted that we play five up front. McLean stuck to a system so his players wouldn't know what has hit them. We could have slaughtered them but it ended up 3–3. Gordon Rae was magnificent and so was Brian Rice. That was with a bunch of lads struggling to stay in the Premier League. They did us proud that day. Afterwards Jim McLean caught me. 'You didn't half fuck us up today coming up and playing like that.' I just told him that was the Hibernian way. I grew up with Hibs as an attacking team who always tried to go and score goals. The Famous Five did it, in the '60s. Hibs were attacking and when Tom Hart was at Hibs that was the way we had to play.

Hibs went on the slide after Tom Hart. He was the best chairman we have had in recent times. There will never be another like him. He was Hibernian FC. We were the best in the world as far as he was concerned. Everywhere we went with him was first class.

We played Hearts at Tynecastle and Hart said to me do you want tickets. Ally and Jackie said tell him Hearts are on £350 bonus to win. So I went to see Hart for my complimentaries. I told him about Hearts' win bonus. He just said 'Is that right'. We got about £200 in those days which was a lot then. On Monday morning I went in to Easter Road and John Fraser said the manager wanted to see me. So I went up the stairs to see Turnbull.

'You, sit doon.'

'What is it boss?'

'What's this about Saturday?'

'Different class, wasn't it?'

'No, not the win. You were talking to Tom Hart. What about this £350 bonus?'

'What about it?'

'I am the manager of this fucking club, no Tom Hart. Yer getting 200 quid and that's it. Don't do that again.'

'Wait the now, boss'

'Oot the door.'

I had to go down and explain to Jackie the Red and Ally that we were getting nowt extra. I had tried my best. However, usually Tom Hart's mentality was if Hearts got a new suit, we would have two new suits. Hibs would never play second fiddle to them. If Hearts got a £1000 bonus Hibs would get £2000.

Throughout my time I got the impression that Tom Hart had a lot of time for Rourkie and me as he knew we were Hibs people. A big blow for him was that we didn't win the Cup in 1979. It was the biggest disappointment of my football career. When we came in after getting beaten I threw my medal away in the changing-room. Greig and Waddell came in and I was standing there. They said to Eddie 'You were unlucky, your team played well'. I butted in: 'Aye, you wouldn't be in here so fast if we beat you.' Turnbull stepped in: 'Calm down, big man.' By now I forgot I had tossed away my medal I was so upset. When I went outside my wife Blanche said 'Let me see your medal.' I raced back to the dressing-room thinking I'd lost it for sure, but Turnbull had picked it up for me.

I suffered that night as a player and a fan. I always felt like a fan when I played Rangers and Hearts. Just ask Jocky Scott who's now at Hibs what I was like at Dundee when ever we played Hearts. They couldn't understand the buzz I got from beating them. Mind you they hadn't the honour of growing up in the Southside of Edinburgh.

The best time of your life is as a juvenile because when you go pro there's a whole different attitude. It is not about enjoyment. It is your job, your livelihood.

Then came my chance to go to Hibs. Stewart Brown, the former *Evening News* reporter, phoned me and said Eddie Turnbull had asked him to ask me if I would be interested in going to Hibs. Well, you know the answer. I was actually in hospital with meningitis when it happened and Dundee got relegated. Dundee's manager Davie White got on the phone. He didn't know Eddie had already got the word through to me. Davie White's exact words were: 'Do you want to sign for the club you have always wanted to play for?'

I'd had great times at Dundee and we had been regulars in Europe. Rookie and Pat used to come up and watch me in those games and I would go down to support Hibs. When I joined Hibs we were still regulars in Europe. One time when we played Sochaux in France we came out after the game and it was pouring rain. There were some Hibs fans there and Tom Hart was shouting for me to come on. But I asked the boys what they were going to do. They said they were going to start trying to get home but they were skint. So I gave them some money. When I got on to the bus Hart asked me what I was up to and I told him. He sent me back with more money, but they had gone. When I got back to Edinburgh I found an empty champagne bottle in the pub with a note saying 'To Big Dode, thanks for the bevvy'. I was daft enough to think I was giving them cash to get something to eat.

I like to think Hibs were and still are a family club, but a big family club. Hibs fans have always had high standards and we must never lose that. When I was at Dundee any of their players would have jumped at the chance to sign for Hibs and it is vital we never stop aspiring to be a big club. Proof of the potential is the crowd we took abroad last time we were in Europe. Over five thousand is more than Aberdeen took to a European final. That says it all about Hibbies. Today I look at myself as a Hibs supporter not as a former player. I've always been a punter and the two most important things in football will always be the punters and players.

CHAPTER THIRTEEN

GREEN GAZZA

As testimonials have become more and more frequent fans have got a bit cynical about the whole business. But in recent years if any Hibs player deserved a testimonial it was Gordon Rae. A sign of how much Gordon was appreciated by his fellow pros was the calibre of the opposition for his big match when Alex Ferguson brought Manchester United to Easter Road. That night the eulogies from his peers in his testimonial programme said it all: 'wholehearted', 'loyal', ' brave', '100 per cent professional', 'honest' and 'he could play a bit'. He was also the only man who could fill Tony Higgins' shorts.

The stamp of the man was when Hibs went through the rough times, Gordon was a permanent fixture whose stability ensured the club kept on an even keel. Unfortunately as has so often been the case at Easter Road when it became time for a loyal servant to leave it happened in rather ignominious fashion. 'I was gutted when it happened,' Gordon says 'and I moved on to Partick. I had spent so many years at Easter Road yet the only person who phoned me to wish me all the best was Dougie Cromb. It's funny though, what Eric Stevenson told me has come true. It's only when you are gone that you will be held in higher esteem by everyone. And I have been touched by how good to me Hibs supporters are.'

Another product of Bonnyrigg, Gordon remembers the big deal as a laddie living near Hibs player Eric Stevenson.

I lived just down the road from Eric and it was a big thing when you saw him in the street. When I joined Hibs, Eric had been away for a few years but there were still quite a few of the big names that I had admired so much still at the club, such as John Brownlie and Alex Edwards. Arthur Duncan was another and it's incredible how long he lasted in the game. I had been spotted playing for Musselburgh Windsor by Hibs scout Johnny Smart and offered training facilities. There were 30 odd boys training there on Thursday nights; among them a few who slipped through the net to Tynecastle, such as John Robertson, Gary Mackay and Ian Westwater. But Hibs never gave them contracts and Bobby Moncur stepped in and scooped them up for Hearts.

I was playing for Whitehill Welfare when Eddie Turnbull asked me to sign for Hibs. At the time I had an apprenticeship at McTaggarts at Loanhead and was attending Esk Valley College, but had no second thoughts about it. I went in to see Eddie Turnbull and he laid out the terms. I opened my mouth to say something: 'I think . . .' when he banged his fist on the desk and said: 'I do all the fucking thinking around here. Now fucking sign this.' That was Eddie for you so I did what I was told. You won't be surprised to hear I still call him boss to this day. But whatever you say about Eddie he was definitely the one who taught me most about the game. He was the best there was tactically and everyone who came across him will tell you that. Even the older pros who had worked under Jock Stein and Eddie would say that when it came to actual tactics and the ins and outs of football Eddie knew more. Now that was some compliment. They would say that Eddie at his peak in the early '70s had two formations: one for playing up the hill and one for going down the slope. Hibs would be 1–1 at half time but Eddie would be on his way to the airport to watch some European team they were due to play, knowing they would do the business and sure enough they would end up winning four or five-one. Whatever anyone said about Eddie he had his own distinct style.

When I first started he would work with young lads like Craig Paterson, Benny Brazil, Stevie Brown and myself in the afternoons and you could still see he loved the game. But I think his enthusiasm for some aspects for managing the senior team had gone a bit. But passing on his knowledge to the younger lads still excited him. I remember one time it was snowing so Craigie, Benny, Stevie and I were in the gym and we had a Hoola-Hoop up which we were trying to knock the ball through. We didn't realise Eddie had come in until we saw a ball from the back of the gym screaming through the hoop. There he was behind us, these big galoshes on. He had literally wellied it with great accuracy. People had said he was the least skilful of the Famous Five. Well if that was true what were the others like? They must have been world class.

Eddie would not spend much time talking to the young laddies, unlike Pat Stanton. When Pat was manager he would sit for a couple of hours telling you stories about the past and they were great to listen to, but Eddie just stuck to purely football whenever he had something to say. The one time he did open up a bit was after the 1979 Cup final and we were on our way back from Hampden after having lost the third game in extra time. As we returned to Edinburgh on the bus Eddie came down the back to speak to a group of the younger players. We were all down but he quietly lifted us. He told us we had done the club proud and the future of Hibs lay with us. It was just what we wanted to hear.

Joining Hibs at that stage in the '70s they felt like a big club which was due to Eddie and Tom Hart. The atmosphere at the club was different in those days and you would only speak to Tom Hart and directors like Tommy Younger and Jimmy Kerr if they addressed you. You were not even allowed up the stairs at Easter Road unless you were sent for. Tom Hart had done so much for Hibs and you could tell he had a real passion for the club and football in general. He was still an innovator and was instrumental in bringing the two Norwegians Isaak Refvik and Sven Mathieson to Easter Road and, of course, George Best. He was a fair man and you knew he would not piss you about. He and Turnbull were close and played golf a lot together. Obviously the good relationship between the two had been good for the club. Both of them had all the players' respect.

When I broke through to the first team I made a dream debut in the league. My first game at the start of season 1975/76 was in the reserves against Ayr United. We won 3–1 and Roy Barry and Jim 'Bimbo' McArthur were to look after me. I scored a goal and was in the first team to play Queen of the South in the League Cup. I did quite well and got off to a good start netting after six minutes but the goal was disallowed.

On the Thursday Eddie Turnbull phoned me at McTaggarts to tell me I would be in the first team pool for Ibrox on Saturday. I was delighted but never thought for a minute I would be playing. Maybe I might make the bench. On the Saturday he announced the team on the bus so I did not really have time to be nervous as he had left it so late. I was only 17 and I remember going up the tunnel at Ibrox and seeing all these players like McLean, Jardine, Parlane, Forsyth and Jackson warming up. They had won the treble the year before and here was I at Ibrox facing them whereas two weeks before I had been turning out for Whitehill at juvenile level. And what a start I had scoring after only four minutes into my league debut at Ibrox. Bobby Smith hit the ball in and Peter McCloy failed to hold it. I followed up and popped it in. I used my knee and that was not the first time I would score with it over the years.

We won 2–0 and the whole experience was unbelievable. That I had scored on my debut was all over the papers on the Sunday and Monday. I had just met my wife a couple of weeks earlier at the dancing in Gala and was due to have a date with her that night. Well I didn't make it as I went out celebrating with the boys in Bonnyrigg. One of her friends said to her on the Monday 'Is that not that guy you've started seeing in the papers?' Margaret did not know what she was talking about and just about fainted when she saw me on the back pages. I had not told her I was a footballer as I thought she'd be after my money. But needless to say she was totally unimpressed as she wasn't in the slightest bit interested in football.

I started as a striker and played there for the most part in my early years with Hibs until Pat Stanton took over. I had never played as a centre half before I came to Hibs. I started off up front and played a couple of games in midfield. Over the years I was to play all over the place but it was something that never bothered me. I was just delighted to get a game. Turnbull tried me at the back on a couple of occasions when George Stewart was injured and I would slot in beside Jackie McNamara. But the big man claims it was he who spotted my potential there when he was on the staff with Pat.

Playing in different positions teaches you a lot about the game. Eddie Turnbull was a man for that so you understood what the different roles were.

These early years saw the turnover of the early '70s team with Brownlie, Schaedler, Blackley and Edwards all moving on. Guys like Jackie McNamara, George Stewart and Ally McLeod were the backbone of Turnbull's last Hibs team.

Jackie McNamara was the leader of the team. He was a great player, but also a lot more than that. Everything he said and everything he did was right. When I became captain I would often think 'What would Jackie do in this situation, how would he handle that?' He was a hard man on the pitch and could handle himself and was an example to the other players. Big George was a real enthusiast and an out-and-out Hibbie. Eddie made him captain and Jackie and he were some duo at the back. Then there was Ally McLeod and the only player apart from him that I have known who had such confidence in his ability was George Best. Ally was arrogant and I fell out with him a few times in my early days as he gave me a hellish time, but he was a brilliant player, and he knew it. Then, as opposed to these three, you had others like Bobby Hutchison who was mental. No other word for it. A good laugh though and not a bad player. Benny was another stalwart of those years and a lot of the stick he got was unfair. You knew Benny could do a job and you could rely on him. Things were brightened up by the short stay of the Norwegian duo Refvik and Mathieson when Tom Hart took on the Department of Employment over work permits. Questions were raised in the House of Commons but they were gone before the rule was actually changed.

Hibs were still involved in Europe but we were knocked out in 1976/77 by Swedish side Oesters Vaxjoe after beating French club Sochaux in the first round. The next season Hibs' first trip was back to Sweden again, this time to play Norkopping. Ernie Walker accompanied us to make sure everything went smoothly after the debacle in Argentina. The SFA did not want a Scottish club making a fool of itself in any way. But Ernie had to fly back when Ally McLeod resigned as Scotland manager.

In the next round we played Strasbourg and lost 2–0 over there and I was responsible for conceding a softish penalty. In the return match we could only win 1–0. However that season was far from over. We reached the semi-final of the League Cup and lost to Aberdeen in extra time only after a freak goal by Stewart Kennedy caught out Primo. Big Mike McDonald stepped down to let Bimbo back into the team. We were to get our revenge over Aberdeen in the Scottish Cup later on that season. First we had Hearts to take care of and that was some match. I ended up enjoying it more than the final. Both big George and I scored as we beat Hearts 2–1.

In the semi-final it was Aberdeen again, this time at Hampden and I scored again along with Ally McLeod to see us through. The final was disappointing as intially I was on the bench as a sub although I came on late in the game. In some ways I didn't really appreciate being in a final. Most players are lucky if they get a couple in their career. Even Old Firm players don't have that guarantee. I was not that long out of juvenile football where I had been in about ten finals a year.

In the first game we had a good chance to win when Colin Campbell was brought down by Peter McCloy but we never got the penalty. In the second game I was on from the start up front with Colin in a 4-4-2 formation. We had worked hard at criss-crossing and the one time it worked I was in the clear at the back post on the six yard line. Colin was in two minds whether to shoot or not and eventually put it past. In the third game we went up after McCloy dropped a cross from me and Tony Higgins stabbed it home. Then there was another chance Colin had to slide the ball square to me to tap in for number two but he shot and McCloy saved. Rangers then went up the park and scored. They then got a penalty and Bimbo pulled out all the stops to save Alex Miller's effort. They went in front then Ally McLeod scored with a penalty as he had done in the semis. So it was into extra time again but poor old Arthur headed a Davie Cooper cross into the net.

Naïvely I thought I would be back and was not too disheartened. And on the way back we got that lift from Eddie Turnbull when he came down the back to share a few words of wisdom. We actually still had to play Rangers that season in the league and it was now about 31 May. Colin and I both scored as we won 2–1 and it only made you think what could have been. Not only would there not be any more Cup finals, but the next time we got to Hampden, this time in the League Cup final in October 1985, I missed out due to suspension. We beat Rangers in a two-legged semi-final with Roughie in brilliant form at Ibrox. But that's where I picked up a booking.

The season after the Scottish Cup final I began to appreciate the highs and lows of the game as we were relegated and got hammered 5–0 in the Cup semi final by Celtic. But although it was a desperate season we were back in our high profile role with the signing of George Best. It was a great move by Tom Hart. It had everybody talking and really aroused interest in Hibs. People would stop you in the street to ask about it all the time. George himself was a great guy. He didn't bring any of the superstar nonsense with him and just fitted in with the rest of the lads. On the park he was still exceptional and some of the things he did were marvellous. Even Ally McLeod would concede that.

On our Christmas night out we went to the 'Persevere' for a meal and George was not drinking. But the following week he went down for Bobby Tambling of Chelsea's testimonial and went AWOL. George did have some trappings of the superstar. He got his after-shave in Paris and it cost about £100 for a wee bottle which was a hell of a lot of money especially in those days. But he would give all the lads a shot of it after they came out the shower. You would have about eight guys queueing up to splash it all over, all going around smelling like George, hoping some of the magic would rub off with the women if not on the park. He was the first player I had come across who had complete faith in their ability apart from Ally McLeod. Both knew how good they were although George had a bit more reason to think so than Ally. But George alone wasn't able to save us as we went down.

Eddie packed it in and Willie Ormond took over. Willie was one of the nicest guys in football and perhaps too nice to be a manager. Peter Cormack had also been brought back and he still had the touch. I don't think people realise what a good player Peter was. Willie also got John Connolly. He couldn't run any more but in the First Divison he could rip up defences. I remember in our pre-season training going up to Elgin and we were sweating away on a roasting day when Willie appeared bawling at us to come over. We went over expecting a rollicking. But he told us we were the best bunch of lads he had worked with and insisted in taking us for a drink in the clubhouse. That was the kind of guy he was, really laid back. Although I say he was perhaps too nice for management he had been successful as his record at St Johnstone showed and he did Scotland proud at the World Cup in 1974.

Willie packed it in just before Christmas that season for health reasons and Bertie Auld took over. Bertie got all the credit for our immediate promotion but Willie had done all the groundwork. Bertie only brought in one guy Billy McLaren and it would have to have been Bertie. We called Billy 'The Rat' and some of the things he got up to were disgusting. He was always mucking around in the showers and changing room. One time he put linament in Tam Hartley's shampoo bottle. Now Tam was totally bald and he was washing his head with this stuff and his head started bubbling up and the skin came stripping off.

Apart from Billy, Bertie made us a harder team to beat. However his true accolade was that he was the manager who did more for team morale than any other. The reason was simple. . . everyone hated him. Who knows, it might have been deliberate? But he really knew how to go over the top. There was the time he made Jackie McNamara walk back from training at Hunter's Hall while the rest of us took the coach. He had accused Jackie of being a prima donna and if there was one player you could never accuse of being a prima donna it was Jackie. I think at that time even the groundsman hated Bertie. So there was a real lift when we heard he got the sack and Pat took over.

The place was bubbling and these were my happiest days at Hibs. Pat brought in Jimmy O'Rourke and George Stewart and we had real Hibs people running the place. There was a superb atmosphere and he started bringing young boys through again like Mickey Weir, John Collins, Gordon Hunter, Paul Kane and Willie Miller.

What people don't appreciate is what Pat inherited. The structure had collapsed from when I started out with 30 to 40 boys training at Easter Road and a big ground staff. Pat had no cash but because of the contacts Pat, Jimmy and George had they got people and ran things on a shoestring.

Now there are young boys coming through again at Easter Road but Alex Miller has had about ten years to build it up whereas Pat was there for only a couple of seasons. What was produced then in such a short time set Hibs up for a good few years.

Alex Miller has also had the full backing of his board. Even under Duff and Gray things went well with Hibs buying Andy Goram and Stevie Archibald, two great assets. These were lively days and it was only really with hindsight that we saw the club was going off the rails. But they pulled the wool over everybody's eyes. I remember in that game against Morton when Andy Goram scored we were warming up beforehand when Andy says: 'Hey Gaz, what are these two ***** doing?' I turned around and there they were taking a lap of honour and they went into the crowd to watch the game. Maybe then we began to rumble this was a bit of an ego trip. But despite all the carry-on in 1990 the club was strong enough to bounce back. Hibs have been through the bad times and the fact that we hung in there was important. Now things can only get better.

CHAPTER FOURTEEN

THE KANE GANG

The Kane gang have to have a place in Easter Road history if only for the fact that father and son have both worn the green and white. Paul's spell was longer term than his father's as he went on for a distinguished career with the club, carving out a role as a top-class utility man. He was also from the same mould as Jimmy O'Rourke. He wore his heart on his sleeve and it was green. Maybe if Paul had a fault it was that he was too close to the fans and at times that brought him into conflict with the management. But if anything that made him even more popular with the punters.

While Steven Tweed and Kevin Harper are finally breaking through from the youth policy it was Paul who led the last crop of youngsters to come through in force. He was the senior member of the Kane gang – Mickey Weir, Gordon Hunter, Calum Milne and Johnny Collins – young players who, out of necessity, had to bear a lot of responsibility over the years when times were really tough at the club. As Kano recalls:

My very first day at Hibs and do you know what I was doing – building the sponsors' lounge for Kenny Waugh. It could have been the end of my career before I even started as I stood on a nail and burst my foot.

I had been signed by Bertie Auld after playing for Salvesen against a Hibs select at Riccarton. Bertie asked me for trials and it was an offer I couldn't refuse. My dad had played for Hibs in 1958/59, but his career was short-lived as he broke his leg in a collison with Tubby Ogston against Aberdeen. My family were Hibs daft and my heroes as a laddie were Pat Stanton and Jackie McNamara. My dad took me to watch Hibs against Motherwell when I was two years old and I caught pneumonia. As you can see I lived to tell the tale and I am still here and still a Hibbie. That gives some idea of how Hibs daft we were at home. If that wasn't enough the school I also went to – St Mary's in York Lane

– was Hibs daft and another great Hibbie, big 'Yogi' (John Hughes of Celtic) was in the year above me. I trained with Meadowbank a bit and Terry Christie lived round the corner. My dad pushed me a little but he knew I didn't have a divine right to make it. In the Salvesen trial against Hibs we won 3–1 and another team-mate, John McGachie, was also to have a short spell with Hibs at a later date.

I joined as a midfielder in 1982. Hibs had just won the Under 18 league with guys like Carlo Crolla, Gordon Burns and Robin Rae. There were actually more guys from Glasgow, but when Kenny Waugh took over a lot of them from the west were let go with the boys from the east staying.

I was grateful to Bertie for signing me but I only worked under him for a couple of months before Pat was made manager. I was in awe of him. Pat Stanton was not just a top man with Hibs but in football in general. Mickey Weir, Gordon Hunter, John Collins and Kevin McKee came in just behind me and we had a great crack together which set you up for later years.

My debut came in a friendly against Swansea City who had John Toshack as manager. I came on as sub and it was some introduction as I was up against Ray Kennedy who was a beast of a boy and gave me a bit of a rough time. Anything would be easy after facing him. My full first-team debut came in the league against Dundee at Easter Road in the replay of a game cancelled because of fog. They let everyone in for nothing and Willie Irvine, Willie Jamieson and I scored.

The usual five-a-side game in training at that time was of the old timers McNamara, Callachan, stopper Stewart, goalkeeper O'Rourke and Pat against me, Mickey, Geebsie, John Collins and Kevin McKee. With Jimmy in goals it was very hard to score he'd just lay himself across the goals. They used to try and knock lumps out of us but we were too quick for them. They were very bad losers.

It is surprising how good the general spirit at the club was considering the cost-cutting that was going on and how Pat had to work against a background of no money. When Pat spoke everyone listened. George was more of a motivator. He and Jimmy would get you going and if you did something wrong George would blast you from all angles and never miss you.

Jimmy was the joker in the pack. He was Alan Rough's personal assistant and had to warm him up and get him going which was some achievement as Roughie was the most relaxed footballer in Scotland. O'Rourke and Rough were some act. I don't know who told the bigger stories. If one told you something the other would have to better it with something more outlandish.

Jackie McNamara and Ralph Callachan were players you looked up to. When Pat left Jackie would always give you advice and pass on tips to you. Big Gordon Rae was another. He was 'Mister Hibs' and a real 100 per center.

At the start I was that keen I didn't feel any pressure, I was just delighted to be playing. But as you get older you get drawn into more things than just the football and can get caught up in the politics of a club. Unfortunately that draws you away from the football side which is what you're there for. When you are a local boy there are also always supporters who played against you at boys club or juvenile level and say you're hopeless. They always remember playing against you and being better than you. Funny though how they're not professionals! But you never get that comparison if you're at another club. The other side of it is that everyone knows who you are and you get a lot of encouragement.

Meantime there were changes ahead at Easter Road as George, Jimmy and Pat walked out. Pat came back for a while but I think he felt he had had enough and needed more backing. But to be honest I was still a teenager and a lot of these things pass you by. John Blackley had been assistant to Pat so the switch over was not a big problem. Maybe John was not quite ready but anybody would want to give it a crack. John made a good move bringing in Tommy Craig. The young boys benefited most from Tommy. He was really good with us and took a special interest. He worked on our passing, control, crossing and finishing and I would say all of us appreciated that later. We were quite successful with Sloop in the League Cup and Cup, but not so much in the league. In the league we suffered because they were building the enclosure on the east terracing and it was an eerie atmosphere to play in and I felt it affected our home advantage in a few games.

At that time Gordon Durie and Steve Cowan struck up a great partnership. I fractured my cheek bone at Tynecastle in the league so I missed the Celtic game which we won on penalties in the League Cup and the first leg at home against Rangers when Gordon Chisholm scored in his debut. I was back for the semi-final at Ibrox and although we lost 1–0 we were through. Roughie was superb and even after Davie Cooper scored from a free kick we were still confident. We thought we were destined for the Cup especially after beating both the Old Firms. But the final was over before we knew it. I remember, in the tunnel, looking at the first three guys in the Aberdeen line-up. It was Miller, Leighton and McLeish. They had been through it all before. As young lads we were a bit overawed especially as it was our first cup final. There's not a lot I remember, apart form a 35-yard shot I had and Jim Leighton making a great save. Then Aberdeen just seemed to take over and we were chasing the game. But one thing that sticks in the mind is the great support Hibs took through.

We also got to the semi-final of the Cup later that season and met Aberdeen again. I had been sent off the week before. Hibs started off well and Johnny Collins hit the bar and if that had gone in it could have been a different game, but again we were well beaten. One of the most pressurised games I have ever played in was under John Blackley at the tail end of the season before that. It was a 'do or die' relegation battle in 1985. Pat Stanton had already resigned after Dumbarton had beaten us at home earlier in the season. We now had to beat them to avoid relegation. Hibs laid on free buses which guaranteed us a tremendous support and we won 3–1. We just could not have afforded to lose that one. I was more worried about that game than any other.

John Blackley left a few months after that and I just looked on another change of manager as a natural occurrence. I had had three managers in four years which is more I suppose than some players have in their whole career. You get accustomed to one manager and his system of play then another comes in. They all have their own ideas of how to play so you have to adapt.

It's funny to think back, but Alex Miller spoke very highly of me when he took over and even told me that he'd tried to buy me when he'd been at St Mirren. Although there was a fair bit of politics around Easter Road over that period there were to be many more highlights. You have to give it to Alex Miller that he got Hibs back into Europe and the game against Videoton must rank as one of the best performances by a Hibs team I have seen.

There was also the small matter of the derby win, Hibs' first in ten years. Eddie May got the first that day and I scored the winner with a header. We felt a win was due as there was a new regime at the club with Duff and Gray taking over and I remember them bringing down the champagne to the dressing-room after the game and everyone giving it pelters.

Andy Goram had just signed and he was an immediate bonus as he just did not like losing. It also meant a lot to me as a local boy especially having had so many defeats or draws with Hearts rammed down my throat. But that goal must remain one of, if not the, most memorable ones I have scored. I went up for the corner and because I wasn't that big compared to some of the others in the box nobody picked me up. I saw it coming over, went for it, met it and sent it into the top corner. It was a great release and you know it's an important goal, an historic one even, because it meant so much to the fans. It was just like Gordon Hunter's goal at Tynecastle at the beginning of the 1994/95 season.

One of the main reasons we got into Europe in the 1988/89 season was because of Steve Archibald, one of the best all-round players I have played with. Up until the time he came to Hibs I had the impression he was a bit of a loner, but there was nothing further from the truth. Once we got to know Stevie no one at Hibs could understand this image he has. He was very much part of the team. He made quite a stir when he turned up at training in his Rolls-Royce. He was full of quality and everyone learned from him. He had great movement on and off the ball and was one of the best I've seen at holding up the ball. He could make and create for others and his 16 goals were invaluable in what was only about half a season.

In the first-round home tie the next season we squeezed through with just one goal thanks to Mitch. I think a lot of people thought that was it, but the boys were outstanding in Hungary and everything went to plan. Funny how wee things stay with you. On the afternoon of the game we had gone for a sleep. Andy Goram was my room-mate and we were woken by talking in a courtyard below us. Down there were Jim Gray, David Duff and in between them on a garden swing was the famous Frank Dougan. Gray and Duff were hardly lightweights but at the sight of big Frank swinging his feet in the air Andy turned to me in amazement: 'I can't believe that swing's still standing.'

The performance that night against Videoton was the best I have seen by a Hibs team. We went out to make sure we did nothing stupid early on and got the best of starts after ten minutes when Mitch laid on a cross for Houchie to head in. After that we were in total control. In the next round against Liege we were unlucky to lose to what can only be described as a goal in a million.

However, not long after, in January 1990, I was to leave Hibs after nine years. I felt at the time I had been there long enough and a change would do me the world of good. I had been playing in a number of positions and while that is good for you as a youngster where you learn a variety of roles it's not so good as you get older. Your form can suffer if you cannot build up enough consistency in your game.

I had also been on month-to-month contracts for about six months. There were a lot of politics at the club and it was affecting my game. I became deeply involved and looking back I probably should not have bothered and just concentrated on my own game. But it is hard when you are born and bred a Hibbie. You just can't help it. When you step away you realise it is probably not worth it. How you are judged by the fans, managers and other players is what you do on the park. And when Joe Royle came in and offered me a midfield role at Oldham I took it. But I had hardly been away from Easter Road when the takeover bid happened. It came as a real bolt from the blue and it was worse because I was away from Edinburgh and did not know how things had been developing. I kept in touch through people I was close to at the Hibs club like George Stewart and Jimmy O'Rourke. I came back up as the 'Hands off Hibs' campaign was swinging into action and I was at the rally at Easter Road. It was just something that couldn't happen. The club I'd supported all my life could not just disappear. I had been born and bred in Leith and Hibs had always been a part of Leith. If Hibs no longer existed it would be like ripping the heart out of the community. Like everyone I was both relieved and delighted when it all fell through.

I am also delighted that Hibs is not leaving Easter Road. There may have been a financial argument for it in some ways but a Hibs supporter just can't imagine Easter Road not being there anymore. There are so many stories about the place you just never want to let these memories go.

When I left Hibs they had a good team and it's got better over the years. Andy Goram was a world beater who should have been getting more caps when he was still at Hibs. I had the honour, or misfortune, of being his room-mate – it depends on how you look on it. He is a character and that's what football's all about having people like Andy around. One of his first games was against St Mirren at Love Street and he was beaten by two looping headers from Ian Ferguson. I thought 'What have we got here?' and christened him 'the dud'. But it did not take him long to make me eat my words.

John Collins was another top-class player. Johnny stayed with my folks when he first came up to Hibs from Gala and he and I have always been close. We grew up as players together. Both he and Andy are different characters but have proved themselves at international level. John has always been more wary of people but Andy will team up with anybody for a laugh. But I always knew John would make it as he was a very determined and single-minded character.

Mickey Weir is another player who is a bit special. He's like me and virtually knows all the same guys as I do and hates the Hearts just as much as I do. His career has been hampered by injury but he still has a lot to offer Hibs. He took Hibs to the League Cup final in 1991 with great displays in the semi and the final. Hibs need him back and he has too much quality not to be used. Having him back will also be like signing a new player. When we were on the ground staff Mickey and I used to clean the stand on Friday afternoons and sing Hibs songs together.

Another special player from my era is Gordon Hunter. He is a quiet, big lad, and probably the worst trainer I've come across but on a Saturday at three o'clock it is another matter. He's some player and anyone who thinks differently should try playing against him. I should set the record straight that it wasn't actually me who christened him 'GBH'. It was Pat Stanton who came out with it at training as Geebsie was running around with his training bib GH volleying people up in the air. Pat was muttering: 'GH . . . GBH more likely.'

These guys – Mickey, Johnny, Geebsie, Calum Milne and Kevin McKee – were all on the ground staff with me and we were all Hibs daft and used to sing the songs in the showers every day. Eddie May was another real Hibbie who went to the same school as me and Yogi and scored in big games for Hibs such as the Hearts game in 1987 and the 4–3 quarter-final Cup win over Celtic in 1986. Brian Rice was another gifted player from that time who maybe doesn't get the acclaim he deserves. But Steve Archibald, as I've said, was the real stand-out and I never appreciated how good he was till I played with him and I am sure every other player who played with him would agree.

But it is not just your own team-mates you appreciate. That is the great thing about football, the lasting friendships you make with guys from other teams. One that springs to mind is John Robertson. We go away back. He played in the same Salvesen team as me and trained with Hibs. We could have saved ourselves some bother if we had signed him full-time back then. But he's just another one that got away.

The important thing about football is there are so many positive things such as the friendship, characters, banter and the supporters. One thing I will always appreciate is when I returned to Scotland to play for Aberdeen. Who should my first game be against but Hibs. It was a strange feeling running out at Easter Road in another strip, but I will never forget the great reception the Hibs supporters gave me.

CHAPTER FIFTEEN

HE'S HERE, HE'S THERE, HE'S EVERYWHERE

A well respected journalist, the late John Fairgrieve, once compared the young Mickey Weir to Puskas and remember John was a Jambo. He may have been a bit over the top but the point he wanted to make was that Mickey reminded him of another era and unfortunately there are too few like him in Scottish football today. Mickey, more than anyone, epitomised the tanner ba' player.

The wee man has had his ups and downs since then, but lest we forget, Mickey was the key man in leading Hibs to their first trophy in two decades as man of the match in the League Cup semi-final and final in 1991. It also makes you despair about some of the people involved in football when you hear that Mickey gave up football at school as people told him he was too small. Mickey says:

But my father told me to keep at it and encouraged me. So I got stuck back in playing for St Augustine's and Portobello Thistle and through that Jimmy McManus got me along to Easter Road. It was Jimmy who also brought Johnny Collins along not long after me. At the time it meant so much to me as all my family were Hibs people and going on the ground staff was a dream come true. There were only three others there when I first started – Kano, Gordon Hunter and Kevin McKee.

That just shows what a shoestring the club was run on at that time. We had no third team and as a result the young laddies got thrown in. I witnessed first hand how short of money Hibs were and how Pat Stanton never had a chance to do what he wanted at Hibs. Despite that, he and George Stewart and Jimmy created a brilliant atmosphere. The four of us on the groundstaff did everything together such as cleaning the terracing and it created a strong bond between us. Jimmy O'Rourke used to always say: 'Remember who you are playing for – the

Hibs. And don't ever forget that.' That meant a lot to me and still does. The longer I have gone on in the game the more I have realised it is a job, but my feeling for Hibs has not changed. You feel it especially badly if you lose a derby game. Ask any Hearts player who is also a supporter and they'll tell you the same. To win means everything. A draw is not too bad, but to lose is a horrible feeling and you can't wait till the next derby to get a chance of revenge.

My first game for Hibs was in a reserve game against Aberdeen and we got stuffed 7–0. They were getting ready for a European tie and were giving a lot of the first team a run out, like Simpson, Cooper, Hewitt, Black and Andy Watson. Pat was calm after the game. There was no bawling or shouting. All he said was: 'Learn from that. That's the sort of quality you have to aim for.'

My first-team debut was another one that I could not forget for other reasons. It was the one against Dumbarton that led to Pat Stanton's resignation. I wondered what I had done wrong and felt quite guilty as though I was to blame. I also felt really sorry. I couldn't believe he'd packed in. As a person, manager and player he was everything. I looked up to him as the king. He had a presence and just had to walk in and look at you in a certain way. In training he was also still some player. He had good men around him like Big George and Jimmy. George was the kind of man who would go bananas and gives us a hard time if things were not going right.

Then there was Rourkie. He had his own way. He was more of a motivator and was the biggest influence on me. In some ways I was similar to Jimmy in size and build. Jimmy brought a bit of arrogance into my game. He was always winding me up saying things like: 'You'll get in the first team before so and so' and 'Are you not embarrassed to clean his boots? You're miles better than him.' I was just a young laddie but as I got older I realised what he was doing to me – building up my confidence. Rourkie could also put a bit of fear into you with just a couple of words. If you were doing well he would tell you, and if you weren't, he also told you. He was very honest. He'd tell us to go out, show our skill, and not be trampled on by anyone.

The three of them knew all about Hibs and would tell us about the club. Pat also said to us: 'You are good laddies and you can go on and do well for the club.' I'm glad to say we proved him right by going on and making the grade. Johnny

Collins, Willie Miller and Geebsie were others who also came through under Pat's guidance. Geebsie broke through into the first team at an early age and he's never looked back since.

John Blackley took over after Pat and he brought a lot of new players to Hibs. He seemed to get a bit more money to spend. He was a hard player and a hard manager, but did well as a manager considering the circumstances. He got us to the final of the League Cup and the semi-final of the Cup. However we lost both to Aberdeen. The semi-final against Rangers was some achievement and big Roughie was magnificent in the second leg at Ibrox. I missed the final though as I had glandular fever and watched it on television in the house. It was really men versus boys and our inexperience showed as they won 3–0. Kano told me they were in the tunnel before the game and big McLeish turned round, looked at the Hibs boys and then let out a huge roar and everyone jumped. Mind you I have always loved playing in big games and always have relished going to places like Ibrox, Parkhead and Hampden.

Probably my favourite game is against Rangers home or away. Although we were by no means a great team we got a few results against them at that time. Games such as the one when Colin Harris grabbed a late winner at Ibrox and when Kevin McKee got jumped when a Rangers supporter ran onto the pitch and attacked him. There was the other occasion when Houchie and I scored in a 2–0 win when Boni Ginsberg was in goal. That night I was walking down Lothian Road when a boy came out of a pizza shop and spotted me. He started roaring: 'Mickey, come here.'

I thought will I, won't I, but eventually went over. He insisted: 'Here Mickey, have a bit of ma pizza.' At that moment he staggered forward and slapped his pizza all over my shirt and tie. That's the fans for you. I had to go back home to my ma's and change again, he almost ruined my Saturday night.

One Rangers game early on in my career that really stands out is Graeme Souness's first game. We were all taken aback at Souness joining Rangers and everyone was looking forward to the game as there was such a build-up. Everyone expected Rangers to win as Souness had splashed out on Butcher, Woods etc but we outplayed them and were 2–0 up at one stage and could have added to our lead before they pulled one back. But Souness showed he was some player, streets ahead of everyone else, with great vision. The way he was pinging passes around you knew he would have a great influence at Ibrox. But then he went and did that tackle on George McCluskey. You could tell it was a bad one as soon as he went in and then all hell broke loose. Everyone ended up getting booked although I wasn't involved at all. I got knocked over and I still don't know who by. Big Schulz – Mark Fulton – was another who got knocked over or who knows he might have taken a bit of a dive. Only big Roughie stayed out of it as even Chris Woods came steaming in from the Rangers goal. I remember thinking 'What is happening here?' I'd gone in trying to pull people apart.

After the game we were jumping about in the showers singing and dancing. But John Blackley just came in and said: 'You've done your bit, now go out and enjoy yourselves tonight.' Poor old Toby – George McCluskey – couldnae as he was up in the hospital. Toby had been brilliant that day and was torturing them until he got savaged. He was never the quickest of players but he had some skill. Nutmegs were his speciality and he used to do them every week. He'd be out on the byeline, kid on he was going to cross and the boy would come running in and Toby would slip it through his legs and over it would come.

It was a pity he was coming to the end of his career but if someone asked me who is the best player I worked with it would be Steve Archibald. He did not need to run about. Archie just knew where to be. His touch was superb and you knew you just needed to put the ball up to him and it stuck. People called him a mercenary but that was utter rubbish. He was a great professional. He'd looked after himself perfectly and would take his training seriously. There was never an ounce of fat on him. He'd had a lot of moves over his career and made a lot of money but good luck to him. On the park he was three moves ahead of everyone else. It was frightening how good he was.

As a youngster, when I first joined Hibs, Ralph Callachan had impressed me. I used to watch him in training. He was poetry in motion and never gave the ball away. As a wee laddie I'd liked Alex Edwards a lot and of course Cropley, Stanton and Rourkie. But Mickey played the game his own way. I don't know if he would get away with it today. But their manager Eddie Turnbull must take the credit and from what I have heard he was very highly rated and ruthless as well. Everyone says he was ahead of his time.

A guy I admired who never played for Hibs was Gordon

Strachan. My build is a bit similar to his and I watched how hard he worked and how he used the ball. Strachan was the sort of guy who would work his way through a bad spell. I consider that his greatest attribute.

As a supporter I never missed a home game. My dad and uncles would take me to the game and we would stand down by the floodlights. The European games were a special treat. One of the games that stands out most although I was just a laddie was the East Fife game when John Brownlie broke his leg. We used to have a bus from the Doocot pub that went to the away games. These were the years when I didn't play on a Saturday afternoon. I played for school on Saturday mornings and Pilton Sporting Club on a Sunday.

It was my dad who kept on at me and told me to stick in as something might happen and it did. At Easter Road Pat and Jimmy kept me going. Pat kept drilling into me: 'Your height doesn't matter. It's how big your heart is and if you've got the skill.'

Although I have not got on well with Alex Miller at times I must say he has also been a big influence on me. He is a great coach and knows the game inside out. I've learned a hell of a lot from him not just about football but about life, such as handling the press and other matters. He knows the game and taught me how to play my position. He is also a manager who knows who the best man for each job is.

My best spell so far has probably been the run up to the League Cup and that was because I never got touched by injury. Both the semi-final and the final were something special. Rangers were clear favourites in everybody's book, but the manager talked us through the way we would be playing. There were a few close things that night but overall we were the better team and I was happy to lay on the goal for Keith just as I was in the final.

Another achievement of Alex Miller was getting Hibs back into Europe. My first European game was against Videoton and I had really bad toothache all the way through it. It came on the night before and the next day the gaffer said 'You cannae play with it.' But I said that I was playing no matter what. It was worth it despite the pain. For two weeks after that I was suffering and my face was up like a balloon. I nearly got sent off that night. I was in absolute agony and that made me a wee bit irritable. We were missing chances and then the penalty came.

Houchie missed it after Snoddy got treatment for an injury. I was getting frustrated and the pain was getting worse. I took a bit of stick in the press but they didn't know what I was going through. I admit I am not the greatest of losers and did swing a boot at someone.

I was absolutely gutted at not getting a start in the second leg. The manager changed things a wee bit as it was a European away tie and tightened things up a bit. Everyone was leaping about on the bench celebrating as we won 3–0 but it was not the same for me. I was spewing and just wanted to get home. I was sick at not getting a game. The gaffer told me I wouldn't be playing because he wanted to hit them on the break which is what happened. The game went exactly as the gaffer said it would. But no matter what anyone says it is never the same for a player if you do not get a game. Everybody wants to play on a night like that. After that everyone was buzzing and the fans were delighted. Jim Gray was joining in and doing laps of honour as if he'd scored himself. He kept patting me on the head telling me not to worry, but I just felt like knocking him out. Guys like him don't appreciate what a player's going through. You have missed what could have been a great night in your life.

Liege was a real killer. I played in the first leg, but again was dropped for the second. I was behind the goals and saying to Goram: 'A minute to go Andy. Come on we can do it.' If it went to extra time we could nick something as they were tiring. Then the boy Albert let loose from 40 yards with his wrong foot. As soon as he hit it I thought 'Oh no, here it comes.' Anderlecht was another great European game when the lads did really well in the first leg but I lost out again after getting sent off; I think I was bit unlucky. I had put my leg up and that was it as far as a Continental referee is concerned. We played well, but they were a very good team, masters at the break-away.

Once again the gaffer prepared us very well for that tie. He works 24 hours a day and every night he's out watching two games. I doubt there is a harder worker in football. He's bought the right players and worked his way through on a limited budget.

During my time in England I was amazed at some of the managers and how little they knew. If you're sitting on the bench here it is an education listening to Alex Miller and I remember I used to pay attention to what Jim McLean or Alex Ferguson would be saying.

In England the man who impressed me the most was Kenny Dalglish. My second game for Luton was against Liverpool and I got taken off with ten minutes to go and I just sat and listened to Kenny Dalglish. They had just bought Ray Houghton and he got the ball and began to dribble with it.

Dalglish was up: 'Houghton, pass it'. He got the ball again and started dribbling with it. Dalglish was up: 'Pass it'. Third time he got it and starts dribbling and Kenny was up 'Houghton, off'. And he had just put him on. He gave him three chances and he was off for running with the ball. That was the Liverpool way, you had to pass the ball.

Since the League Cup season things have not gone so well for me because of injuries. The season before last was the worst. I went to see a specialist and he told me I had to rest till the end of it or my career would be over. Since then I have been building my way back to fitness. It's been a long slog but I am sure I can reach top form with Hibs again. I've missed out a lot as the boys have been flying at times, but my return at the end of the season could not have been sweeter.

In all these years I have been at Hibs I had never played on a winning side against Hearts. It just shows you how bad our record has been. It's something that's hard to explain to fans as there have been so many games when we should have won easily, but somehow it ended up a draw or they scraped a win. I was at Luton when Kano's header earned us a 2–1 win in 1987 and I was injured when Archie scored in the 2–1 win at Tynecastle. On the third occasion, John Collins and I were on the bench when Eddie May scored the winner in 1989. Then at the beginning of last season (1994–95) on the Friday I said to Ted I had a feeling that we would do it the next day. I find it very hard to watch Hibs although it's no problem watching other games. I was very tempted to break my general rule and go to Tynecastle, but I didn't. Geebsie went and did the business and then we beat them in the next derby at Easter Road when we could have run riot against them. So the last derby of the season meant a lot to me. I had not been in for a long time and it could not have gone better if I had written the script myself. To score and be involved in the other two was something else especially after they had gone ahead. It's not before time that we turned the tables and I've a feeling this is the start of something for both me and Hibs.

CHAPTER SIXTEEN

A CASE OF GBH

Cometh the hour, cometh the man. It was a captain's duty to end Hibs' dismal derby run and Gordon Hunter duly fulfilled it in September 1994. Twenty-two games without a win were wiped away in one glorious moment when the man who's more used to dishing out damage at the back appeared at the far post to get on the end of the flick on from Dave Beaumont to Mickey Weir's corner.

It was one of these occasions and Gordon knew instinctively the ball was coming to him:

I don't know why but I could just tell. That's why I moved into that position at the back post. When I hit it I was less than six yards out and the ball could have gone anywhere, but I'm deadly from that range! What made it so special was it was at the Hibs end and I was delighted later to get a picture from a photographer of me running over and jumping up towards the fans. I think that says it all. I had never scored against Hearts but it was worth the ten-year wait to do so on such an important occasion.

I am from Wallyford originally but my uncle who lived in Restalrig took me to my first Hibs games as a boy. I was doing well with Musselburgh Windsor when I went on S-forms to Hibs. John Butler and Jimmy McManus were instrumetal in my signing. When I actually went along with my dad to sign on at Easter Road Bertie Auld was the boss, but the very next day he got the bullet. I was just a kid at the time and I was a wee bit worried about what had happened, but it never affected me at all. So my experience of Bertie was short and sweet. I do remember he was very loud.

Pat Stanton took over and a year later I went full time. George Stewart told me Pat used to say: 'What do you think of the big red-haired laddie?' George would say: 'I think he's got it.' But Pat would say: 'I don't like the way he runs. He runs awfie funny.' But George must have turned him round and I believe Pat had the last word, telling George: 'If it doesn't work out heads will roll.'

I have heard that Jackie McNamara tells a story of me clattering him in training early on and I was only wearing sand shoes. Well I suppose I got a reputation quite young for being, let's say, 'wholehearted'. We used to get sheets back from the SFA about our bookings and wee notes for me like, 'This lad should settle down a bit'. Mine was as thick as a telephone book compared to everyone else's. But I think my approach was one of the reasons I broke into the first team at such an early age – I was only 16 coming on 17. I could look after myself which is very important for a centre half. People say it is a position young boys don't break through into early. It's easier as a winger for instance.

When I was young I played up front, wide on the right but I broke my leg when I was 13. When I came back in I played in defence. At that age you worry a bit about what it will be like but my dad drummed it into me that I had to get stuck in and not be afraid. Since then I have never been the type to shirk a tackle and I would like to think my reputation isn't deserved these days. With experience you learn not to be so rash. But one thing I never get booked for is mouthing off. I think it's a piece of nonsense. As a defender you are going to pick up bookings anyway, it's the nature of the job. So to get others for a bit of lip is plain stupid. You'll also never change a referee's mind once they've decided something. Have a quiet word and he'll respect you for it. But temperamentally I'm not the type to get worked up so that I end up shouting. The gaffer will say nothing bothers me; I'm a happy-go-lucky guy. Even in the last two seasons I've been sent off twice and on both occasions it was against Mark Hateley. I'm not a squealer but I didn't deserve either of them. He came across me both times and fouled me. As I went down I stuck my arm out one time and the other time I grabbed him. Needless to say I got the red card. Maybe I should take it as a back-handed compliment that he finds me hard to play against and resorts to a bit of fouling. But the last game we weren't getting too much at Ibrox as Gordon Durie had fouled David Farrell for their first goal. Anyway I think anyone who can remember seeing my last red card on television will see what I am saying. But it is all part of the game and there's no point complaining about it. Mark Hateley is very difficult to play against and he is a big strong physical player with a lot of pace and skill.

In my early days on the ground staff Kano and Mickey Weir were a year ahead of me and there was Kevin McKee and Calum Milne as well. To me the main man then was Kano. He was a great friend and would do anything for you. As a 16-year-old I really looked up to him and he could talk for hours about Hibs. There had been a big clearout not long before I started so there was just this small group. Today there are at least a dozen on the ground staff and a bigger pool of reserves. The senior players at the club at that time were Jackie, Gordon Rae, Bimbo, Roughie and Ally Brazil. They treated us all the same. I was straight into the reserves and I remember the match-day programme praising me for my display at Celtic Park. They said I was the top man so it was a big boost.

Not long after I started I got sent off in a reserve game at Ibrox. Pat Stanton came in at the end and said: 'Dinnae worry about it. It might no be a bad thing.' At the time I didn't understand what he meant. I was still only 16. But as I got older I realised there was lot in it. You are going to get sent off sometime in your career so it may as well happen early on. Learn from it. I think he also saw that I'd look after myself, but I'd be more careful in future. Rangers' Dave Mitchell who was a right big lad, kicked me off the ball so I whacked him. The ref turned round and saw me so I was off.

In those days Jimmy Thompson took us on a Tuesday and Thursday night. But when I was in the reserves I was training with the first-team squad, unlike today where the young lads are off on their own. In some ways it brought you on quicker. No disrespect to the gaffer now, but I think playing with senior players you learned a lot and you learned it quickly. Guys like Jackie would compliment and tell you not to take any shit. There was also never a dull moment especially with guys like Alan Rough around. The club was struggling financially and there were big problems with the board but the atmosphere among the players was fantastic. My first-team debut came against Kilmarnock when I was 17 alongside big Gordon Rae in the League Cup in 1983/84.

When Pat Stanton left soon after it came as a surprise to me. I didn't know what was happening behind the scenes with Kenny Waugh. But there were signs things were going wrong.

The kit would not be washed every day and you would have to fight to get a top. All that has changed since Alex Miller took over. My first Premier game I played alongside John Blackley. I got on really well with him although some of the players didn't, especially when John became boss.

My weakness in those days, and some might say it still is, was my passing. People like Pat, Tommy Craig and Alex Miller have always told me you've got to know your strengths. The boss says 'Get it and give it wide to players who can play.' That's what I have tried to do, stick to simple things and in that way I can make myself a better defender.

We were a young team that got to the League Cup final in 1985/86. I was only 18 but the second leg of the semi-final at Ibrox sticks out. Davie Cooper scored but apart from that Roughie was brilliant, but big Gaz got booked. Schulz played in the final alongside me but it was really over too quickly. We missed big Gordon, one of our more experienced players. He was one who knew his strengths exactly and would play to them. He was brilliant in the air, a good, strong tackler and had great presence.

Alan Sneddon was a great pro with whom I played for years. He really looked after himself well. Snoddy was a good laugh as was Kano and there are still stories he won't admit to. Johnny Collins was coming through and you knew then you don't get much better than Johnny. He was another that really looked after himself. Another top class pro with loads of skill. Gordon Durie and Steve Cowan had a great spell together up front. Jukie had great pace, strength and could score goals. Steve Cowan didn't do a lot but stick it in but that was all we needed from him.

Tommy Craig helped the young boys a lot at that time and we thought he would get the job after John Blackley left, but he came in on the Friday and told us the team but he wouldn't be there: 'You've a new manager.' That's how we heard Alex Miller had got the job. We didn't know much about the gaffer except that he was boss at St Mirren. But straight away it was clear he knew what he was talking about. Not long after he took over we went away to a friendly in Seville. When we came back he went through every player giving a rundown on our strengths and weaknesses. Not one of us could disagree with what he said. In hardly any time he knew us as players. He was spot on with me. 'Passing poor, could do better.'

Over the years he has said to me that I should be challenging for an international place but I think my problem has been I never really believed it. Even when I was playing well I didn't have that confidence but last season being on standby I realised how close I could be. When I take a look at the players who have won caps I realise what the boss is talking about.

When the gaffer took over he wouldn't take any nonsense. Things began to change in little ways with the kit. We used to go in and the first in got the best gear. If you were late you could be out in just a T-shirt in the middle of winter. Now we had our gear with our numbers on it so no one like Kano could be nicking your gear. It was freshly laundered on a daily basis; before it got cleaned once a week. The boss is still quite distant, but he does have a laugh with the best of us at times. Over the years he's mellowed a bit and will sit and chat after training, but you always know not to cross a line with him.

He made some really good first buys in Graham Mitchell, Tam McIntyre and Doug Bell. I still enjoy playing alongside Mitch if Tweedie's out injured and feel I have a good understanding with him. Mitch is a quiet family man, but he's always in brilliant form when we have our nights out. Big Tam was a smoothie and quite fancied himself. I thought we were a really good combination in the League Cup year. A lot of supporters have asked me why we got rid of him and I think they have a point.

The real character in those days apart from Kano of course was Andy Goram. It was no surprise they ended up as roommates. I knew Andy from the Under-21 squad and thought: 'What's this guy doing playing for Scotland with an accent like that.' One thing about Andy is he'll never change. He's an outstanding goalkeeper. There's the story of Goram introducing me to the drink after the Videoton game but once he went we got a surprising replacement in Budgie. Steve Archibald was another good buy. His Rolls-Royce caused a stir especially next to Kano's Lada. Kano loved Stevie and wanted a Rolls after that.

It was players such as Archie who got Hibs back into Europe. Mitch scored in the first game at Easter Road then came the 3–0 win over there. We had a wee reception after the game and everyone was on a high. The Videoton players joined us even though they'd been beaten. Our goalie turned round and suggested we went somewhere else. I'm not a drinker but he encouraged me to have a few champagnes. He's made up a few stories since about me singing. The next round against Liege was a killer. We should have gone a goal up but Houchie missed a penalty. Then they scored a wonder goal over there. Gareth went to close the guy down but he let loose from 40 yards with his left foot.

One of the biggest pains over the years has been our derby record which has been shocking. There have been a lot of draws but that's not the point. After a while maybe something crept into the back of our minds but when we went in to each game we thought we'd win. Some games we'd been slaughtering them and should have been three or four up. But then they'd go and sneak a goal. There's never any ill-feeling between the players off the park and when you bump into them up the town you always chat. Wee Robbo has some record and is very sharp in the box. Every time he scored in the derby as he was running back he'd say: 'There's another one, big man.'

The boss tried everything to break the so-called jinx. He took us away which he would not normally do. He tried not bothering about the game and ignoring them. He would really play down the hype in the press. He also tried getting us all hyped up. But in the end it is the players crossing the white line who have got to do it. And when it finally came it was an unforgettable experience.

The derby record was one of the few lows since the club had got back on the rails after the 1990 takeover bid. I was away on holiday at the time with a few of the lads such as Calum, Danny Lennon, Billy Findlay, Willie Miller, Davie Nicholls and Chris Reid. Somebody had phoned home and was told about the takeover attempt so Danny Lennon went and got a paper. There it was splashed all over the *Daily Record*. Sitting on the beach trying to take it all in was too much for us. We just couldn't believe it could happen. A lot of money was spent on phone calls. When Duff and Gray had first taken over we had thought a lot of things were going to happen. I had signed a four-year contract and was confident things would go well and then came the share issue. That was the beginning of it. A lot of changes followed after the whole business and one of them was Andy Goram's transfer. Not surprisingly we struggled in the next season, but things took off again in 1991. Johnny Collins and Kano were away too.

But getting Murdo Macleod was a boost. He had won so much with Celtic and had played in Germany and as an internationalist. His experience was useful for the Skol Cup run. To be honest I didn't start that season thinking we would win the cup but by the time we got to the Rangers game everything had clicked. Maurice Johnstone hit the post and gave us a scare. Budgie would always talk about when he dropped the ball at my feet but I didn't clear it properly and Pat McGinlay came rushing in to punt it clear. There were a few dodgy moments that night but Budgie was pretty sharp. Budgie was some boy. Everything you've heard about him is true. He's a real eccentric. He lived in Durham and would come up by train and had a wee moped to take him to the training ground. He was some sight arriving with his helmet, goggles and goalie's gloves. One time he was really upset and we asked what was wrong. Somebody had tipped his moped on to the rail track. He was a fitness fanatic and liked to tell us about when he went down to Leeds with Newcastle. As they went in the gym door was open and Vinny Jones was on a bench doing weights with a ghetto blaster. Budgie went over, turned it off and said: 'Hey son, move over and I'll show you how it's done.' Budgie slammed on the full range of weights and started to pump away.

Goalkeepers are some lot. Roughie was a bit of a lazy trainer but loved playing as a striker. Andy was the same, he liked to play out of goals. But Budgie was just into goalkeeping. Budgie would get mad with the young lads if they didn't train properly and give them a real mouthful. He was a real perfectionist which showed in the bust-up with the manager at Airdrie. Budgie would bring his own jersey although he got the sponsor's logo put on it. The boss insisted he wear the club jersey, but Budgie was adamant his jersey would save us one goal a season. Its special material helped the ball stick more. That was Budgie for you.

Whatever you think of him, he played his part in the League Cup winning team. The scenes coming back from Hampden after we beat Dunfermline were incredible. That day I thought I had missed out on my chance. The night before the clocks had changed and I turned up at Easter Road over an hour early. I had come along extra early anyway but there was no one about. I had a terrible feeling at first but slowly it dawned on me. It was one of the longest hour's I have spent. The thing was that I went and did the same thing in the final in 1993. That evening after we'd won the cup things were calmer than after the semi-final. Then we had really gone and celebrated in 'Fingers' where the place was jumping, full of Hibbies. But with the final we knew we should win and everything was a bit of an anti-climax after the reception we got coming through Edinburgh. It started at the Maybury and went on all the way along to Princes Street, down Leith Walk and to Easter Road and the crowd there. I don't think even Rangers and Celtic in Glasgow would get the crowd we got that night.

The only disappointment was we qualified for Europe but I missed out on the Anderlecht tie and had to listen to the game in Brussels on the radio. The big aim is to get Hibs back there and I'm sure we will with a manager like Alex Miller. The manager is 100 per cent football. He eats, sleeps and breathes it. You almost feel sorry for his wife and now two of her sons are footballers. His attitude starts with the preparation which is very thorough. He goes over the opposition analysing each player – how they will play, their set pieces etc. We have one big team talk and he has always said from day one he will never stop anyone from saying their piece. At times I have had a love-hate relationship with him and he gives me a hard time but later I realise it is for my own good. He does not slag you just for the sake of slagging. He is just wanting me to do myself justice. And I look at the Scotland squad and think 'Why I am I not in it?'

Jocky Scott has begun to take more of the training since he has joined the club and some of us were a bit apprehensive about Jocky's reputation but he can have a laugh with us. But as everyone will tell you there is a great spirit among the lads. Darren's the loudmouth in the dressing-room with always something to say, probably too much at times as is obvious on the park. Michael O'Neill's another one. He's a really intelligent guy and is so quick with the one-liners.

He's also very careful with his money! He shared a taxi back with me and Gareth from the team's night out in Hamilton last season. When it came to splitting the fare three ways he had only a quid. 'But I bought the crisps,' he said. He had actually bought three packets before we got in the taxi. That was his contribution to a £50 fare.

Gareth is a really good guy who took a while to settle but now he is married and happy. The gaffer always says Gareth is one of the best bargains he ever got, costing about £20,000. Ted's some boy – always grunting, not just on the park, but you hear him at it during the team talks. My current partner at the back, Tweedie, is doing really well. A lot was expected from him at first because he was a big lad but last season he improved 100 per cent in putting himself about. He's come a long way. Then there's the wild man, Willie Miller. There's been a huge difference since he married and settled down. You see Willie on the training park and he's brilliant. Maybe a wee bit of that composure goes on the park but the confidence will grow with the years.

Mickey's had his problems but now he's back. With injuries and contract problems behind him, he's a different player. Pat McGinlay is another who has done so well when you think he was a free from Blackpool. Joe T, the Italian stallion, is another comic, but you get the last laugh if you remember what he looked liked when he first joined Hibs with hair down to his backside. Jim Leighton has been a brilliant addition to the squad, but his gear has to be seen to be believed. Ted's as well. Now Ted's trying but Jim doesn't give a toss about that. And I must say Davie Farrell's been a welcome addition if only for the fact he has taking over from me as the one likely to dish out GBH.

CHAPTER SEVENTEEN

THE WRIGHT STUFF

Few players could ever have settled at a club as quickly as Keith Wright did when he joined Hibs in 1991. It was one of the worst kept secrets in Scottish football that the Dundee player was Hibs daft. So Keith was starting off on the right foot anyway but his barrage of goals as Hibs stormed to the Skol Cup final won him a place in the Easter Road hall of fame.

It comes as no surprise, then, that Keith's role model as a lad was none other than one, James O'Rourke esquire. What Keith's ma might have said if she knew Jimmy, like we knew Jimmy, who knows what might have happened. But Keith received his indoctrination as soon as he was old enough when his father took him and his two brothers to see Hibs.

We were at every game, home and away, and my hero when I started watching was Jimmy O'Rourke. The way he played and the goals he scored did it for me. Since I've signed for Hibs I've met Jimmy and been able to tell him. The first time properly was in the run-up to the Skol Cup when I did a preview in the *Sun* along with Jimmy. I told him then that I had idolised him as a boy. I think he was quite flattered. Apart from the terraces I first came across Jimmy when I was on S-forms at Easter Road. Jimmy trained the young boys and he was perfect for the job. He was just the right mixture, serious but also really funny. He was brilliant with kids. I was 13 when I first started and I don't think I would have picked up so much if it hadn't been for Jimmy. I was so eager to learn from my hero. Hibs released me when I was 16 and Jimmy phoned me the day after. He gave me encouragement and told me to go on and prove them wrong: show that I could make it as a pro. There was no way he said I should chuck it. I have always thought a lot of him for doing that.

It gave me a lift when I was down. I played with Melbourne

Thistle Under 18s and a few clubs knocked me back before Raith came in when I was 17. Meantime I worked for five years in Gumley's estate agents in Hanover Street. I was four years at Raith, but always wanted to go full time. The chance came when Jocky Scott signed for Dundee; little did I know we would both meet up again at Hibs. When Jocky came to Hibs I told the boys what a good addition he would be. Any reputation he had was wrong. Training at Dundee with Jocky was second to none, especially if you were a striker. With him and Drew Jarvie all we got was crossing and finishing. Since he has come to Hibs the training has been brilliant and all the boys are raving about it. He and Alex Miller get a lot of respect. There is no mucking about as they won't stand for that. They'd come down on you like a ton of bricks. I enjoyed my days at Dundee and we had a good team. But players began to move on – Tommy Coyne to Celtic, John Brown to Rangers, Tosh McKinley to Hearts, the manager as well. We got relegated and the club slipped a bit. I wanted to get back into the Premier Division. When Hibs were going through the takeover problems I never thought I'd be able to come to Easter Road.

One of the games that sticks in my mind with Dundee was when we beat Hibs 4–0 at Easter Road in 1989. Every time I played against Hibs with Dundee I raised my game. It might seem strange to some fellow supporters, but I wanted to prove that I was good enough to play for Hibs. I did the same against Hearts to a certain extent. I wanted to prove to Edinburgh people I was a good player and also I've always liked beating Hearts.

My dad and brothers probably always wanted a 3–3 draw when I played Hibs with me getting a hat-trick. Eventually when Dundee agreed to let me go I never thought Hibs could afford the figure they were wanting. I was shocked when they came in. Angus Cook told me 'If we don't get promoted we'll sell you.' I sat tight when clubs began to move. I knew Aberdeen were interested and I thought I was heading for Pittodrie. Then Alex Miller phoned me from out of the blue. I had only ever met him at Largs.

The minute I knew Hibs were interested I was set on going to them. Dundee were looking for the most money. I think they offered the same money so I got a choice. It was brilliant coming back and meeting people. For the first few months my wife Julie and I lived in her grandad's house right in the middle of

Gorgie. It was great as I was still staying there when we won the Skol Cup and could walk about with my head up. Right from the word go the Hibs fans were behind me. I know I have been very lucky because in my second season I went through a sticky spell but the fans never turned on me. If that had been another player they might not have been so lucky.

In my first season we started well in the League Cup and I had scored in every round against Stirling and Ayr before we met Kilmarnock in the quarter-finals. It was a great atmosphere at Rugby Park as Hibs took through a really good support. Despite losing a man – Willie Miller got sent off – we won 3–2 with Murdo, Pat and myself scoring. Then it was Rangers in the semi-final. It probably ranks as my favourite Hibs game. The whole build-up to the game was part of it. We were just supposed to be turning up to make up the numbers but we had prepared very well and before the game in the changing-room we knew we were ready. Although the score was only 1–0 that night we could have won by two or three and we outplayed them for long spells of the game. It was a bit special and I got the only goal.

Mark McGraw challenged Andy Goram and wee Mickey picked up his punch out. A lot of people said Mickey went to chip it in, but it was a tremendous cross. The wee man has great first touch and I knew he was trying to find me. There were two Rangers players on the line and I could see them separating so I decided to place it in the middle. It all seemed to be in slow motion. Only half an hour had gone, but that was it. There was an unbelievable support through that night just as there would be at the final.

Afterwards in the dressing-room we were celebrating like we had won the cup. We knew then we could only throw it away. There was also a lot of pride in the way we had gone about beating Rangers. The lads went back to the Piano Bar in Frederick Street that night and it was full of Hibs supporters. They too felt we had won it already. A lot of my mates were late in for the game and they told me when they heard the cheering outside as they were running up to Hampden that they thought Rangers had scored.

The biggest thing among the players now that we were facing Dunfermline was that we could only throw it away. Hibs hadn't won a trophy for so many years and we couldn't have a better chance. To get beaten by Dunfermline would live with us for the rest of our lives. We would never get a better chance. To come away from Hampden with nothing was more in our minds than anything else. We wanted to make sure of a professional job and that is what happened.

You could never call the final a classic. It was not a great performance. It was a question of making sure we got the right result. The first half was a shocker and the boss asked us at half-time if we wanted to leave Hampden without the Cup. At the end of the day it was wee Mickey's magic again that got us the penalty and got me the goal. He won the man of the match award. Tam and I got all the praise for the goals and I got the praise for scoring in the semi-finals, but the wee man was the unsung hero. He was definitely the man in the two games. Throughout it all the wee man was his usual self, staying in the background keeping quiet, but he won us the Cup.

One of the greatest nights of my life was coming back to Edinburgh. I knew it would be brilliant going back into Edinburgh on an open-deck bus, but I never imagined it would be as busy as it was from the Maybury, right along to Princes Street and down Leith Walk and up into Easter Road. Hopefully it will happen again but it was hard to take it all in. When we got back to Easter Road it was a full house. I just didn't want to leave the park or for any of it to end. We wanted the party to go on all night. On the way through Edinburgh I was looking out for people I knew along the way and spotted a lot of my mates on top of bus shelters. They were making sure I didn't miss them.

Through that game we qualified for another one that I won't forget. I had always wanted to play in Europe and had heard it was different, but didn't appreciate how much until I experienced it myself playing Anderlecht. The build-up and the atmosphere are something special and are definitely the tops for any footballer. Playing foreign opposition is what everyone aims for. An added bonus about my first shot at it was that Anderlecht were a top club in Europe and there are not many who come bigger than them. What was different for a start, at home the Dunbar Road end was packed with Hibs fans which made a difference. Then flying over midweek was special with thousands of Hibs fans coming with us. Their stadium and first-class facilities made me feel at the end of it that I wouldn't mind a bit of this every year. It's a big disappointment we did not achieve that in the two seasons following. That night we were so keen not to let anyone down and gave it our all. I always remember Darren being inches away from connecting with a cross and we could have been 2–1 up. I was disappointed with my own performances and felt I should have scored at Easter Road. When we pulled back to 2–2 I hit the underside of the bar but the ball came down on the line.

Other good memories are a couple of Premier Division hat-tricks, one at Tannadice when we won 3–0 and when we beat Dunfermline 5–0 at Easter Road. One of my best goals was one against Kilmarnock with my right foot which is a bit of a rarity. Mickey flicked it on with his head and I hit if first time on the volley. We've missed the wee man recently. When he's on song we really motor. But he came back in at the end of last season and in the best of games, helping us win the derby 3–1. He not only scored himself but set up my goal.

It's a joy for a striker having players like Mickey, Kevin McAllister and Michael O'Neill laying on chances. Breaking the so-called jinx in the derby was a great feeling. I had no trouble beating Hearts when I was at Dundee so it was a great disappointment in recent seasons at Hibs as I know as a Hibs supporter how important it is to win these games. I'm sure any of the boys will back this up but we really could not believe how we didn't win about half of these games. I had scored three times in derbies but in the big one at Tynecastle I was out injured and just about knackered my leg again jumping up when Gordon Hunter scored. After the game I made my way down and had a big smile on my face. Just as I was going in to see the lads some Hearts fans tried to have a go at me and one spat at me. But the doormen grabbed me in time.

The manager was still very serious, going through the post-match team talk when I barged in without thinking. I was so pleased. All the lads burst out laughing and I went round shaking all their hands. Just then I felt we had to put an end to this run. We've gone on and done it now winning three of the derbies last season and I scored in a winning Hibs team, thanks to the wee man.

I've got to say there is a great atmosphere at Easter Road, unlike other clubs where you get a lot of cliques. There is none of that at Easter Road. Even although there are a lot of guys from Glasgow we all get on really well. There's a lot of laughs and the biggest joker's got to be Darren. He's dishing out stick all the time and I must admit he's good at it. Michael O'Neill's not far behind. Jackson's always going on about me and Gareth having big chins – the chinforce of Scottish football. But it's all just to take pressure off himself. He's always slagging Michael about his gear. He went to Italy once on his holidays. So if you ask where he got something it was always in Milan although it looks more like he got it at the Barras.

But one of the best laughs we have is Joe T's impersonations. He takes over on nights out and his best one's of Darren. He's got the wee squeaky voice down to a tee and puts on wee fake sideburns. He's also really good at Alex Miller but I better not say too much about that for Joe's sake.

What Darren and I are aiming for along with Gareth is to score together regularly. We tend to have scored in patches ourselves but would like to combine it so it happens at the same time. It should happen between us because he likes getting the ball short and his touch is brilliant. I like to get it behind defences. I would say we are well matched as a partnership but we have to work on it more. On paper we should do better together than we do.

A big bonus to me in coming to Easter Road was having Alex Miller as the coach. I have worked under five or six managers and he is definitely the best. Tactically he goes into great detail and he has proved in the last few years that we are a difficult team to beat. Hopefully we will continue to score more goals. We have had an unfair reputation as being negative but if you look at the players he has signed like Darren, Kevin, Michael and myself that surely says something. Some of our play last season was really entertaining. I would say he's the best manager in Scotland and it has helped Jocky joining the club just working with strikers such as Darren, Gareth, Graeme Donald and Kevin Harper. One thing Hibs fans can be guaranteed of is that the manager is totally committed to football. Believe it or not he has lightened up a bit since he first came to Hibs according to long-termers like Mitch. It's like night and day, he says. So you can imagine the boss must have been some taskmaster before. He's obsessed with football and goes home and watches it to all hours. Somebody asked if anybody had seen a certain European game and the boss said: 'Aye, it was on Eurosport at 1.30 a.m. last night.' If he's not out watching a game or working at the club he's home watching football and picking up ideas.

I would like to go into coaching when I finish and the boss

has been a great help to me in every sense when I was getting my coaching certificates. I would stay behind and work with the young boys and the boss would show me things: what I was doing right and what I was doing wrong. Of course I'd love to coach with Hibs. Meantime I intend to win more honours with the club before I pack it in and hope to get a taste of Europe again.

CHAPTER EIGHTEEN

OOH, AAH, JACKSONA

After spells at Newcastle and Dundee United, Edinburgh boy Darren Jackson returned to his roots to play for the local side and with it has come a late breakthrough into the international ranks. With it he has built a rapport with the Hibs support that brings to mind the Alan Gordon syndrome. He never started as a Hibbie, but this is how he will be remembered in years to come. However DJ was another who was almost written off because of his stature.

When I was at Trinity as a boy Terry Christie, who was the deputy head, once said he thought I would never make it as I was too wee and too thin. However he obviously revised his opinion as I went to play for him at Meadowbank.

I know there have been a few rumours about who I supported as a boy. I was more interested in playing but let me make one thing clear I was never a Hearts supporter. It's true I was a mascot at a Hearts v Alloa game in 1978. That was just after my school, Leith Walk primary, had won the league, but it was the sort of thing you wouldn't turn down for any wee boy. Robbo told me they just missed out by 12 hours in putting it in the Hearts programme before the game at Tynecastle when Geebsie ended the 21 game run. But let me put it this way: my favourite player as a boy was my cousin Lawrence Tierney who played for Hibs and who has since moved to America to play for Phoenix in the indoor league.

An early part of my career I'll never forget is my spell at Newcastle. There were great players there such as Gazza, Peter Beardsley, Mirandinha and Paul Goddard. It was some experience playing with Gazza as the Rangers players will find out this season. I had him up in Edinburgh a few times from Newcastle and all I can say is he is a great guy with a heart of gold. I took him to Hamilton to watch Meadowbank in the Cup and we went through in the team bus. But during the whole game Gazza just sat and watched mad Fergie, the supporter. He never looked at the game once. It was unbelievable. All he was interested in was Fergie. He loved him and wanted to go and meet him. But that's Gazza for you. One thing for sure is that if he had not had his injuries I think he would have been the best player in the world without a doubt. He was a genius.

When I returned to Scotland my first goal for Dundee United happened to be against Hibs. This seemed to set a pattern although it would be the other way round when I moved to Edinburgh as my first goal for Hibs was against United.

You always remember these goals and the one for United came from a shot from Maurice Malpas which Andy Goram dropped. I was following up and just tapped it under him. A few minutes later a ball came through and Andy came out and clattered me. He obviously wasn't too pleased at me. When the chance came to move to Hibs I jumped at it. A lot of people thought I just wanted away from United and to move back to Edinburgh, but that's not true. I believed it was a good move coming to Hibs because they had won the Skol Cup. Considering what Hibs had been through in 1990 it was a tremendous achievement. I thought the club could only go from strength to strength. The first year it didn't work out as well as I thought but I still knew it was the right move.

I rated Alex Miller very highly as a manager. He's been through the bad times but he lifted himself and the players to believe in themselves and go on and win the Cup. That shows great character.

One example that convinced me I had made the right move was playing Anderlecht in the UEFA Cup. They are a top quality European side. The season after they played us they were in Milan's group in the Champions League and drew twice with them. That gives some indication of the sort of team they were. I don't believe we got the credit we deserved for our performance in that tie. If that had been Rangers or Celtic it would have been a different story. Alex Miller told us their manager had pulled him aside after the game and admitted they were the luckiest side to still be in the UEFA Cup.

In the first game there was a terrific atmosphere at Easter Road and we got off to the best possible start. I hit a shot the keeper failed to hold and Dave Beaumont of all people was following up in the six-yard box to score. We probably became a bit too defensive after that and let them back into the game.

They got a dubious penalty when Budgie was judged to have pulled a man down. He swears he never touched him, as you would expect from Budgie and Degryse scored. Their top man Van Vossen got their second with a clinical finish as he sprang up to clip a lob over Budgie. He was the one who really impressed me. He was playing virtually on his own up front and was an outstanding player.

Mickey getting sent off only spurred us on as often happens when you're down to ten men. At that stage I had a chance when I blasted over when I could have put it in and unfortunately we would pay for it in the second leg.

But we at least got an equaliser when I flicked a cross from Mitch through to Pat McGinlay although there was a bit of dispute whether Gareth following up got to it before it crossed the line.

We really had Anderlecht under pressure that night and I don't think they were too used to it. The crowd at Easter Road was going crazy and although I had played a few games in Europe with United I had never experienced anything like this.

The second tie was a bit special. We trained in their stadium the night before and it was a beautiful place. I really like these enclosed stadiums it adds so much to a ground. It would be great if they could do that at Easter Road at some stage in the future as part of the overall redevelopment.

In the lead up to it we were a bit nervous as we were away against such a quality European side. But the boss kept reminding us about what we had done at home against them. He believed we could beat them. We knew they would have a go at us early on and although we lost a goal after five minutes, the defence was superb that night and regrouped really well.

We had got a real lift when we walked out on to the park. I had never believed there would be such a big Hibs support. It was almost frightening. To our credit we didn't fold after losing an early goal although I would say most people expected us to. We had to get an equaliser and I was the one to do it after a quarter of an hour. I remember seeing Joe T storm up the left and send a ball and Hammie cut it back from the right near the byeline. I moved in ready to receive it and stuck it under the keeper. You could tell from my celebration that scoring that goal was some feeling. It was absolutely tremendous.

From then on they had more possession and we had to work hard for everything we got. I must say Calum Milne was outstanding that night. His role was to sit in, block and make passes. But all of us played out of our skins. I almost got another when Joe again broke up the line and crossed. I made a run to the front post but a defender grabbed my shirt. I was unable to connect properly and could only get a toe to it and the ball went across the face of the goal. If he hadn't pulled my shirt I would have had no problem sticking it in and the way we were playing I am sure we would have held on. But that's part of the game.

If you look at their team more than half of them were in the Belgium squad in the World Cup in America. But they got a fright that night against a team they thought it would be easy to beat. At the final whistle we were very disappointed. In a way we knew we had lost it at Easter Road giving away two goals at home. But I don't think Anderlecht believed a team could work so hard as we did over two games.

As we went off we clapped the fans and went in for the post-match talk in the dressing-room but as soon as we were there we wanted to get back out onto the park to show our appreciation. The fans were as good as we were that night. They gave us such a lift. Even the Anderlecht fans were applauding the Hibs fans. I liked that. It's what you want in the game. But back at the hotel things were very quiet. A couple of beers and then it was off to bed. Despite everything we had lost the tie. Okay it was only on goal average but that often makes it even worse. That Anderlecht game and goal came at a good time. We'd got knocked out of the League Cup but I had just started to score nabbing a penalty in our 3–2 win at Parkhead and scoring a special one against Dundee United.

That goal against United was the start of something. People say I must try harder against United and that I have a point to prove, but that's not true. I try just as hard in any other game. If you were to pick my top three goals they would probably be ones against United. The one in the semi-final at Tynecastle was the most special because of what it meant. The other two were the ones when I smashed it into the top corner at the Dunbar Road end and the lob last season (1994/95).

I had never scored for Hibs until that United game in 1992. By the time we reached the semi-final in 1993 Davie Bowman said to me: 'You cannae get a bet on you. You're a certainty to score.' Yet I hadn't scored in eight games before that game. But score I did. I know I went a run of eight goals in nine games against them, but really I would just like to score every week. I hope Jim McLean believes that. Someone said how delighted I looked when I scored my first goal against United but it was because I had scored my first goal for Hibs and had nothing to do with getting one over my old club.

Another football mystery I just can't explain is our derby run in recent seasons. In the second derby I played in, when Hammie missed the penalty, I don't think I have ever played in a game when my side has given the opposition such a doing. We could have won by so much, but it ended up a draw. It just seemed to be one of those things. It was only after ten derbies that I have played in that we finally beat them. But in at least five of the nine previous games we were the better side. We just couldn't seem to score, but when they got a goal we would think 'Here we go again'. It was heartbreaking for the players and we know the supporters were suffering.

The pressure got worse as it was mentioned every time in the press the derby game came around. It was the same thing at Dundee United when it came to Cup finals at Hampden. When I played for United in the final against Motherwell I went out just not being able to see how we could be beaten. It was the same in derby games. When ever I went on the park I honestly went out thinking we'll beat Hearts and I know the other players thought the same. Every time we lost it was a crushing blow. The worst one for me was when we got beaten 1–0 at Tynecastle and I got sent off in the tunnel.

When we did finally beat them it was an incredible feeling. But, to be truthful, the first half of that game was probably the worst we have ever played in a derby I'd been in. We were simply shocking. We just couldn't get possession or get out of our own half. The second half we improved a bit and they ended up being beaten. The boss was trying to keep us calm when we got back to the dressing-room . At the end of the day it was only three points, but it was a great feeling having finally put the hoodoo or whatever you want to call it behind us.

I was jumping about as the boss was trying calmly to give a team talk, going over how we'd played as he usually does. But the best moment of all was about to happen when the door burst open and in walked Keith. He was the happiest man in the world. It was disappointing that Keith wasn't playing. He had scored a few against Hearts and if anyone deserved to be playing that day it was him.

When the whistle went that day I was away over to the fans

and could have ended up in the crowd celebrating with them, but a linesman dragged me away. Just as well I suppose, but it was something I wanted to share with the supporters. But you have to give it to Hearts that they had held their nerve in the derbies, although in most games I had played in we had been better. Our attitude now was that it was up to us to go on a run and make sure it was two in a row. We did that in the next derby at Easter Road and I thought at one stage we were going to run riot after Michael and I had put us two up. Although we fell back in the New Year game the last derby was another good result coming from behind to win 3–1. Wee Kevin and Mickey were a bit special that day and Keith finally scored in a winning derby which was a nice touch. In that game as well we could have got a few more. So winning three out of the four was not bad. However each game is still three points and you win things by beating other teams. The derby is very important but it is more for morale and the way the fans feel.

After we broke that poor run there were no celebrations that night. We had a game on the Tuesday so I was baby sitting but I got a knock on the door about eleven o'clock from a Mr Robertson who had come round for a wee chat about the game.

It was a pity we never went out as I'm sure it would have been a really good night as there is a great atmosphere at Easter Road among the players.

I like to think my partners up front, Keith and Gareth, while not the biggest strikeforce in Scotland are the biggest 'chin-force'. We have a good laugh about it in the dressing-room where Michael O'Neill's probably the quickest wit around. He has a really funny sense of humour and is a smart guy. We're great pals, having been at Newcastle United and now Hibs together. Wee Kevin McAllister is also another one and if you ever crack a joke Kevin's ready with the comeback. Jim Leighton is great for team spirit as we all get a laugh at his gear. It's got to be the worst in the Premier Division. But you could not meet a nicer guy than Jim.

Everyone knows what he's been through in his career and how he bounced back. To pick yourself up as he did shows strength of character. The boss is also due a lot of credit. Most people thought it was not a good move but they have all been proved wrong. He's the best signing in Scotland for a free trans-fer and the way he regained his Scotland place says it all.

Billy 'Effing' Finlay was another joker. I once mentioned

Billy's vocabulary in the match day programme and he gave me pelters as his mum never knew he swore. Joe T's another comic. His impersonations are better than stuff you see on television. He does Alex Miller, big Martin Ferguson, wee Jimmy McLaughlin, Denis Law and Chic Young. He's brilliant at it. When we have our Christmas night out Joe will get up and do a turn for the boys and that's always the highlight of the night.

There is a good atmosphere behind the scenes and big Martin and wee Jimmy come in on match day and do a job gee-ing everyone up. Most of their work is done with the kids, Martin in the west, Jimmy in Edinburgh. A man I had a lot of respect for was Andy Watson. He was very good but Jocky Scott has come in and done a lot. He complements the boss well. Jocky has taken a lot of the training and has his own ideas. As Jocky was a striker himself everything is geared to the strikers. Even the defenders enjoy it – the attacking side of the game. And Jocky was not at all the gruff character some people said he was. He's very chirpy and if we are struggling for strikers I tell you Jocky could get a game. He's brilliant. He never gives the ball away in training while the rest of us do.

I must admit that although I give him a load of stick in the dressing-room , Keith and I are the best of pals. I did know him a bit before as he was in the year above me with Melbourne Thistle. Keith also played at Dundee when I was there, but since I came to Hibs we've got very close. He's a different class of guy. Gareth is a quiet lad, but another great guy. The three of us get on brilliantly and there is never any animosity between the three of us about who is getting a game.

The sharpest I've ever seen Keith move was not on a football pitch. In the close season before last we went to Tenerife. Keith had been carrying this rucksack everywhere throughout the holiday where he kept his money and a few of the boys had given him their passports to hold. At the airport he nipped off to the toilet. Wee Kev was sitting next to me and asked where Keith was and I told him. He says: 'Come on.' We went down to the toilet and Kevin says: 'Run the taps.' Meanwhile Keith was on the throne with the *Racing Post*. There was a gap at the bottom of the door and Keith's bag was in view. Wee Kev rolled his sleeve up, put his arm under, grabbed the bag and we were out of there in a flash. Seconds later you saw this guy running through the terminal trying to haul his trousers up chasing a thief. There's no way Keith could have wiped his bum. It was some sight not just for us but all the other passengers. The look on his face when he realised it was a set-up was priceless. It was a five-hour flight back and I tell you Kevin and I laughed the whole way thinking of Keith coming out of the bog.

There is a really good closeness between us. We don't have to be out with each other all the time, but when we do we have a great time. The harmony can only help us on the pitch and we all feel we can only get better as a team.

I want to end my career with Hibs and win something. I missed out on the 1991 Skol Cup win and I want to be part of scenes like there were when Hibs came back to Edinburgh that night.

Breaking into the Scotland team has been a terrific boost to my career but my proudest moment at club level was leading Hibs out at Easter Road against Leeds United as captain. It was a tremendous honour. As a striker, and the way I moan a lot, I never thought I would be captain of a club. But when I did it was a big moment. I only hope there are bigger occasions lying ahead for all of us.